RAINY DAY FUN

by
Karan Gleason

illustrated by Vanessa Filkins

Cover by Vanessa Filkins

Copyright © Good Apple, Inc., 1987

ISBN No. 0-86653-408-3

Printing No. 987654321

GOOD APPLE, INC.
BOX 299
CARTHAGE, IL 62321-0299

Dedicated with love to my daughters,
Shari and Shelly,
two exceptionally creative children
and especially my husband,
Art,
for his constant encouragement and love

TABLE OF CONTENTS

A WORD TO TEACHERS AND PARENTS

The activities offered in *Rainy Day Fun* are a springboard for a creative teacher to celebrate rainy days—or any day. Children need to be actively engaged in the learning process. They need to have concrete experiences and effective teaching to foster their intellectual development.

Rainy Day Fun is designed to help you generate enthusiasm for learning experiences for children in K—4th grades. You can use this resource book and the activities herein to make your teaching a new and exciting experience. A rainy day can be fun when you have this book from which to draw ideas.

You will find within suggestions of places to go on rainy days and how to make a walk in the rain educational as well as fun. Teaching techniques are integrated with creative and stimulating games and projects, arts and crafts, and puppetry. Other ideas include bulletin board suggestions, simple crafts, easy-to-follow recipes, as well as awards to create an atmosphere in which learning is fun.

This book will stimulate creativity whether you are celebrating rainy days inside or outdoors. Some of the projects can be done individually, as a class, or even at home. *Rainy Day Fun* is a useful tool whether you're a teacher, a parent, or involved in a home-school program. Its goal is to make learning fun and challenging and to meet the needs of students with differing abilities.

Each of the book's nine units has its own theme and introduction. You can choose one unit each month of the school year to supplement other lessons. Each unit contains a "Making Books" classroom project geared to the theme of that unit. Be sure to note in unit one the instructions for assembling these books (p. 9).

Children are eager and enthusiastic to learn. They look to you as a vital source of knowledge and guidance. *Rainy Day Fun* will help you in your "teacher" role to guide children to become successful learners and to encourage them to discover the world about them. Have fun on those drip, drop, drizzly days!

PUDDLE JUMPING

There are fun and creative things to do on a rainy day. Be sure all the children have on boots and raincoats and use umbrellas if needed. Sometimes it's fun to be outside on a rainy day after the storm is over or while it is misting.

RAINY DAY WALKS

NATURE ALPHABET WALK
Have the children take plastic bags along on this walk. Tell them to find objects starting with the letters of the alphabet (*acorn* for *a* or *rock* for *r*). Give them a time limit to find as many objects as they can from the alphabet.

NATURE MOBILE WALK
On this walk each child will need a plastic bag to collect items of nature such as wood or driftwood, moss, shells, rocks, pinecones, etc. Let these items dry and later make a mobile from them.

A mobile is a moving sculpture that hangs balanced and free. Attach strings, yarn or clear fishing line to the nature objects. Tie the strings at different levels to a wood, wire or cardboard base. Hang the mobiles so they can turn freely.

SEARCHING FOR RAINBOW GLOBES
On this walk have the children look at glittering drops of water on flowers and leaves and especially on the grass. Each drop is a rainbow globe! Notice the different colors in every crystal. Rainbows and colors were created for our enjoyment and fascination.

COLOR TOUR
On this walk have children take a pencil and paper (if they can juggle the pencil and paper with the umbrella)! They choose a color, such as red, and see how many objects they can spot with that color on them. Make a list of those objects.

CREATIVE SPLASHING
The children must have their boots on for sure for this walk! Let them have some fun splashing in puddles, being careful not to splash their clothes or others. They might like to ride their bikes through the puddles if it is not raining too hard.

SPIDER SEARCH
Look for spiderwebs on this walk. Have the class look near the ground and in taller weeds and bushes. Gently touch the web with a pencil or a stick to see what the spider will do. Is the web sticky? Does the web break easily when touched?

CAPTURE A SPIDER'S WEB

If you would like to "capture a spider's web" for the classroom, take along black enamel paint and white construction paper.

When you have found a good spider's web, stand back three to four feet from the web and spray quickly, with a back and forth movement, both sides of the web with a thin coat of black enamel paint. Don't try this on a windy day. If you spray too much, the web will tear or sag from the weight of the paint.

Quickly place a piece of white paper against the web. Curve the paper first in the center of the web and straighten it out very carefully along the sides. Let the web dry on the paper.

You might like to read *Charlotte's Web* by E.B. White to the class.

OBSTACLE COURSE

Set up an obstacle course on the playground, using cardboard boxes, barrels, milk cartons, tires, ropes, etc. The class can help you decide where the obstacles should go and what the players must do when they get to them. Jump over? Run around? Crawl under? When the obstacle course is set up for the children, they try to go through it as fast as possible without upsetting the objects.

WHAT TO DO WITH THE ITEMS YOU COLLECTED ON YOUR RAINY DAY NATURE WALKS

NATURE KEEPSAKE BOX

To make nature keepsake boxes, use the items that were collected on the nature walk. The items might be pinecones, rocks, shells, moss, driftwood, acorns, etc. Let the items dry. Then glue them onto a shoe box cover in any design.

Spray paint the items after the glue dries. Children can keep all their special treasures in their nature keepsake boxes.

SHADOW BOX

Have each child bring from home a box that is fairly shallow, such as a handkerchief box, a tie box, or the cover of a shoe box.

Paint the box and let it dry.

Arrange outdoor objects on the bottom of the box to make a design. Lift each object carefully. Put a little glue on the bottom and gently press the object back into place.

Let the glue dry. Hang the shadow boxes up around the room as a memory of a rainy day nature walk.

NATURE PUPPETS

You can make nature puppets from pinecones that are glued to branches by gathering the needed items during a walk. Use seeds, acorns, pods, and leaves for the features and hats. Use moss for hair. Glue it all together and create your own nature puppets.

NATURE GAME

Each child could use one or two items that were collected on the nature walk for this game. Have a variety of items and let them dry first.

Then have each child put his items in a large paper bag or box. With eyes closed, each player gently feels an object inside and tries to guess what it is. The object is then pulled out. Keep passing the bag or box around until all the objects have been pulled from the bag.

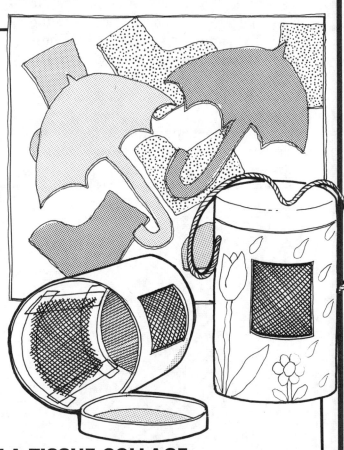

BUG CATCHER-KEEPER

Here's a container to make to keep all those delightful creepy bugs in that children love to collect.

Take it along on your rainy day walks.

Cut some windows in an empty oatmeal box. Cut pieces of screening or nylon netting a little larger than the windows. Tape the screening inside the window openings on all four sides of the windows.

Paint or decorate your bug catcher-keeper and let it dry.

Poke a hole in each side of the box near the top. Thread a long piece of yarn through both holes for a handle. Tie the ends together. Keep the lid on the box when the bugs are inside.

BOOTS AND UMBRELLA TISSUE COLLAGE

Cut out boots and umbrella shapes from various colors of tissue paper. Using a brush, cover a piece of construction paper with a mixture of glue thinned with water. Next lay on several shapes (overlapping some) and smooth them down with your hand. Make several layers, brushing glue over each one.

INDOOR NATURE GAME

Each player writes the word *nature* across the top of a piece of paper, each letter heading a wide column.

N   A   T   U   R   E

Players take turns as the leader. The leader calls a letter from the word *nature* and a category (such as flowers, birds, fish, trees, forest animals). All the players write down as many names from that category, starting with the letter chosen, as quickly as they can. The player with the most names is the new leader.

LOLLIPOPS

2 cups sugar
½ cup water
1 cup light corn syrup
½ tsp. food coloring
1 ½ tsp. flavoring

Grease a cookie sheet with margarine.

Lay Popsicle sticks on the cookie sheet— leaving lots of space between them.

Mix sugar, water, and corn syrup in a pan. Put in the candy thermometer.

Boil over medium heat until the candy thermometer reaches 280°. Do not stir.

Remove from heat and add flavoring and coloring.

Immediately pour the hot liquid over the sticks, covering ⅓ to ½ of the stick. As the liquid cools and starts to harden, you can' shape the lollipops into boots and umbrellas.

See if children can think of other rainy day shapes for their lollipops.

Makes twelve to fifteen lollipops.

RAINY DAY OR
ANY DAY SNACK MIX

Choose any of these to make a snack mix . . .
pretzels
sunflower seeds
any nuts or peanuts
almost any kind of dry cereal such as Cheerios,
    Wheat Chex, or Rice Chex
small marshmallows
raisins
uncooked oatmeal
sesame seeds
granola
carob chips
chopped dates
coconut
dried banana chips

APPLE-CHEESE KABOBS

1 apple, peeled, cubed
¼ cup lemon juice
1 cup cubed cheese (Monterey Jack or cheddar or mozzarella)

Dip apple pieces in lemon juice to keep from turning brown. Alternate cubes of apple and cheese on skewers. Wrap in plastic wrap and chill until ready to take on a rainy day walk or eat afterwards.

How does Amy keep dry? Connect the dots and see.

MAKING A BIG SPLASH IN SECOND GRADE

Preparation:
Make large umbrellas, raindrops, red boots, and puddles from construction paper and attach to the bulletin board. Make a border of raindrops. Attach appropriate lettering.

Use rainy day symbols to border the good work papers or any rainy day poems the class writes.

A fun book to read to the class that tells the different kinds of umbrellas and their uses and explains that no two are alike is *Umbrellas, Hats, and Wheels* by Ann Rand, Harcourt, Brace and World, Inc., 1961.

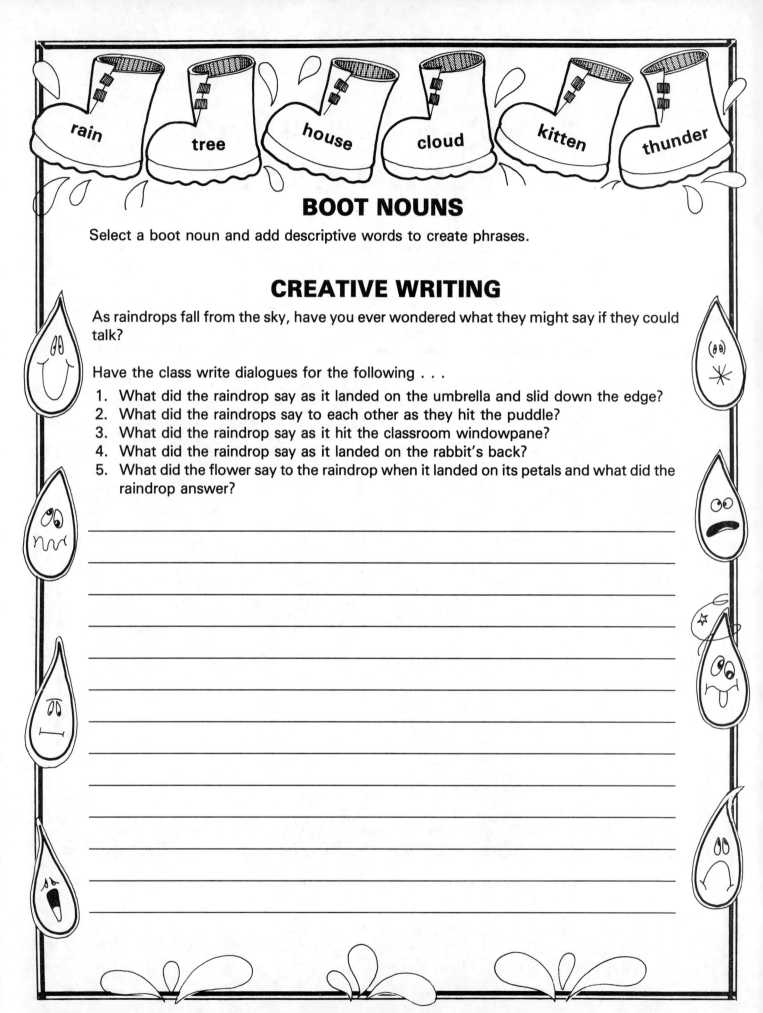

BOOT NOUNS

Select a boot noun and add descriptive words to create phrases.

CREATIVE WRITING

As raindrops fall from the sky, have you ever wondered what they might say if they could talk?

Have the class write dialogues for the following . . .

1. What did the raindrop say as it landed on the umbrella and slid down the edge?
2. What did the raindrops say to each other as they hit the puddle?
3. What did the raindrop say as it hit the classroom windowpane?
4. What did the raindrop say as it landed on the rabbit's back?
5. What did the flower say to the raindrop when it landed on its petals and what did the raindrop answer?

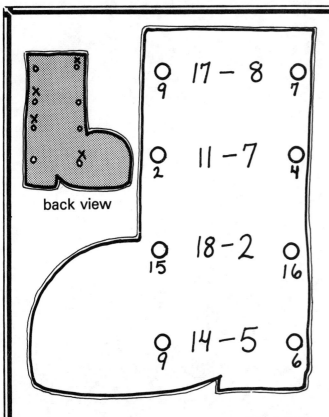

back view

MATH BOOTS

Materials needed:
red construction paper, paper punch, felt-tip pen

Purpose:
to review math skills

Procedure:
Make rubber boot shapes from red construction paper. Place math problems in the center of the boot as shown in the illustration. Have two possible answers for each problem. Make some holes with a paper punch and laminate the boot for durability. The student looks at the math problem and puts a pencil in the correct hole. An "X" on the reverse side will indicate the correct answer.

THINK CREATIVELY

Challenge the children's imaginations with this rainy day question: How many things can you wear to protect yourself from the rain?

MAKING BOOKS

Making books is a fun classroom project. Making books keeps the children reading! Making books keeps them writing, too!

Draw the umbrella shape on a duplicating master and duplicate an adequate supply. Students take sheets, as needed, write on them and cut out. The covers can be made from construction paper or poster board. The student simply traces around one of the pages of the book he has created. Details can be added to the construction paper cover with pen, paint, crayons, etc. A back cover can also be created.

Pages can be put together either by stapling or using brads and a paper punch. For more durability, laminate the cover of the book before binding.

Students will be careful with the books because they created them. Add them to the classroom/school library. These books will be among the favorites for several years.

On each page draw and tell about places to visit or things to do on a rainy day. When the class does something on a rainy day, add this to their books.

PLACES TO VISIT ON A RAINY DAY OR ANY DAY

Sometimes it can be fun to go on an outing on a rainy day. There are many places to visit and things to do. A walk in the rain can be fun, but tell each child to wear boots, a warm coat or rain jacket, and take an umbrella.

Library

Fire Station

Florist

Bakery

Farm

Museums or Historical Buildings

Food Factory

Newspaper Press

Police Station

Post Office

Pet Store

Construction Site

Airport

Subway Ride

A Zoo

A Harbor

A Tall Tower with a View

A Railroad Station

Ferry Ride

Children's Theater

Indoor Swimming Pool

Sports Events

A Local TV Station or Weather Bureau

Planetarium

Educational Demonstrations or Tours

10

UMBRELLA MAZE

Find your way to the handle.

START

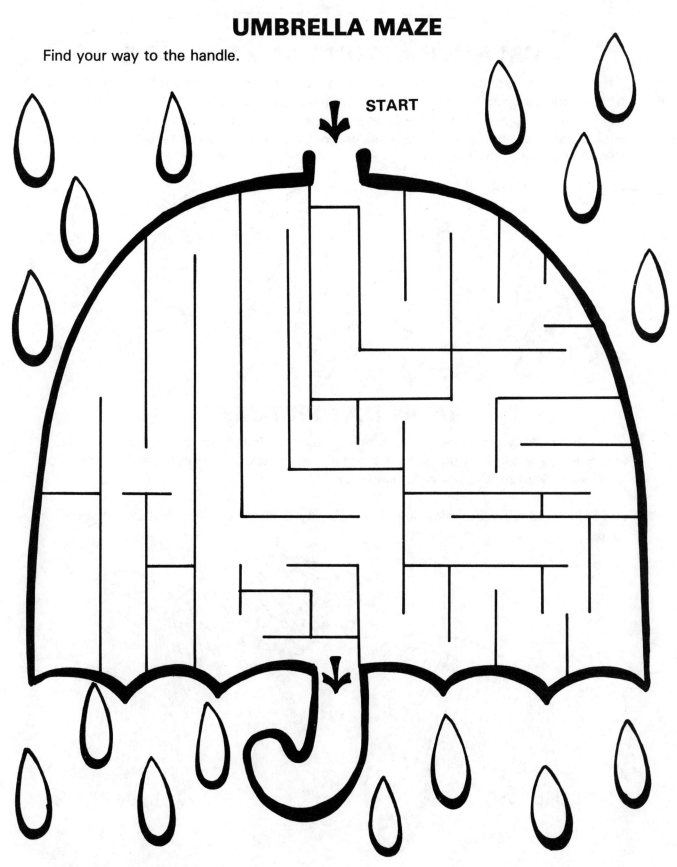

Suggested Reading:
Taste the Raindrops by Anna Grossnickle Hines, William Morrow & Co., Inc., New York, 1982.

CREATIVE WRITING AND DRAWING

After one of your puddle jumping adventures, come back to where it is warm and have the children hang up their raincoats and umbrellas to dry. Tell them to write stories about their adventures and to draw pictures of themselves. Include their rainy day clothing, such as raincoats, umbrellas, and boots and what they did or saw on their adventure that they told about in their stories.

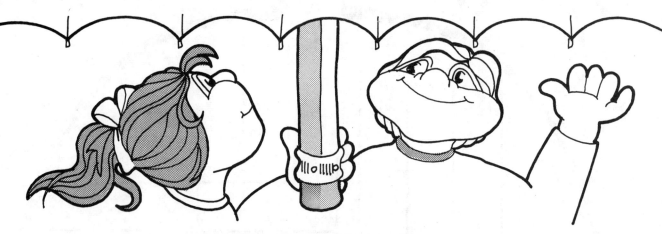

RAINY DAY PICTURES

Give each child two or three paper cupcake holders. Have them fold the holders in half and glue one side down on light blue construction paper, making umbrellas. Use pipe cleaners or yarn for the umbrella handles.

Have the children create rainy day pictures using these colorful umbrellas as the center focus.

Suggested Reading:
Rain Drop Splash by Alvin Tresselt, Lothrop, Lee & Shepherd Co., New York, 1946.
A perfect book to read to restless children on a rainy day.

MUD BETWEEN MY TOES AND FINGERS

Rain makes us think of mud puddles. Mud can be a mess, but in this unit it will be fun to work with squishy things between your toes and fingers. The children will learn many fun ways to use their hands and feet in "muddy" activities, games, recipes, science projects, crafts, etc.

FINGER LICKIN' PAINTING

Materials:
instant pudding
slick paper
clean paper

Try finger painting with instant pudding! Make up a package of instant pudding according to the directions on the package.

Spoon it on a slick piece of paper or shelf paper that has been placed on top of newspapers. Create your own patterns and designs.

You may add food coloring to vanilla pudding. Finger lickin' good!

"FEET" PAINTING

Materials:
finger paint
slick paper
flat pan
wet sponge
newspapers

How about having the children finger-paint with their feet?

Spread a large piece of slick paper or shelf paper on top of newspapers on the floor.

Pour paint into a flat pan. The children will dip their toes in the paint or make prints with their whole feet.

Have them clean off their feet with a wet sponge.

BUBBLE PAINT

Materials:
½ cup soap flakes
½ cup water
food coloring
shelf paper
newspapers

Using a mixer, whip the soap flakes and water until thick and foamy. Put the fluffy mixture into small containers and add food coloring. Mix with a spoon.

Put the shelf paper on newspapers. Spread the bubble paint on the shelf paper with fingers. The bubble paint will be thick like frosting and look like snow. Have the children paint a creative picture or a design or make clouds, snow scenes, or fluffy animals.

The pictures will need to dry overnight.

FINGERPRINT CREATIONS

Tell the class that everyone's fingerprints are different. There are no two alike!

Have the children put their fingers on a stamp pad or in some paint and press them carefully on paper. They can add to their prints with colored marking pens.

They can make cartoons or animals, birds, people, or insects. Fun to use as stationery!

Materials:
stamp pad or paint
paper
colored pens
fingers

BIG SHOES TO FILL

Fill this space with a list of reasons that your dad is special to you and your family.

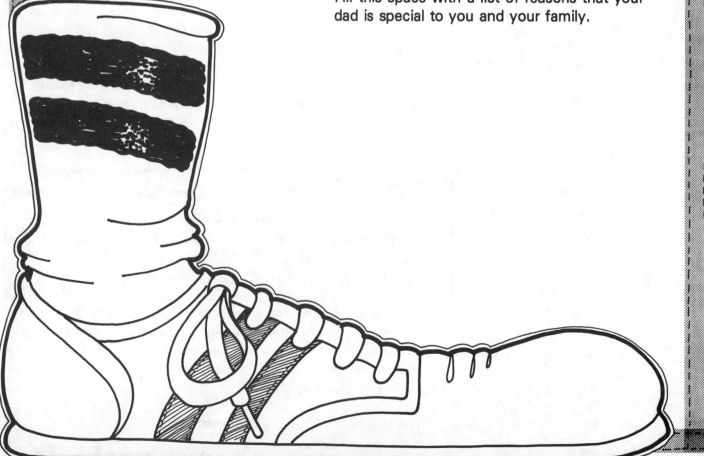

SPECIAL FEET

Help each student trace his foot with a pencil on a sheet of lined paper. After each foot shape is cut out, have each student write a word or a sentence on the foot outline that tells why his foot is extra special.

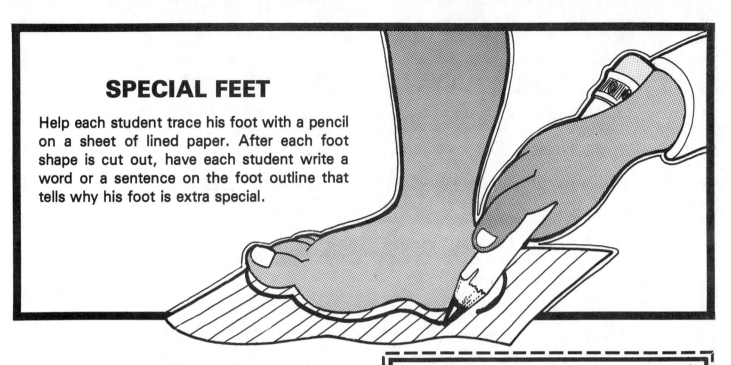

COLORING CONTEST

This coloring contest will be fun for everyone. Give students a simple picture to color. Everyone takes off one shoe and sock. The pictures must be colored, using only the toes and feet! A time limit of three to five minutes should be set. Post all the pictures so everyone can vote on the best ones. This is sure to get giggles and laughs from all the kids. Award the appropriate certificates.

Uncoordinated TOES AWARD

TO: _____

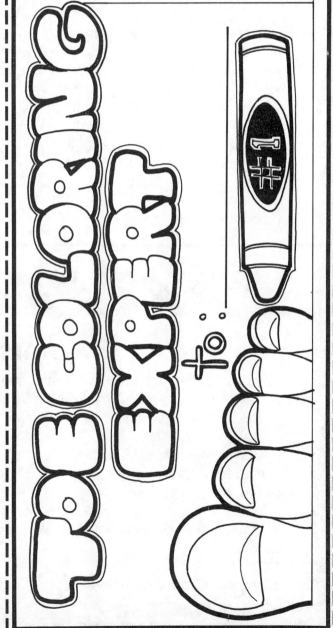

TOE COLORING EXPERT

HOW MANY FEET? 0, 2, 4 OR MORE

Hold a class discussion on the number of feet (legs) on animals. Children can indicate numbers by using fingers to show their guesses. Hold up pictures or name animals and let the children indicate the number of legs.

After counting feet, students might want to draw pictures of four animals. One should have no feet, one with two feet, one with four feet, and one with many feet.

Can any conclusions be drawn after this discussion?

Birds have how many feet?
How many feet do animals have?
Insects have how many feet?
How many feet do fish have?

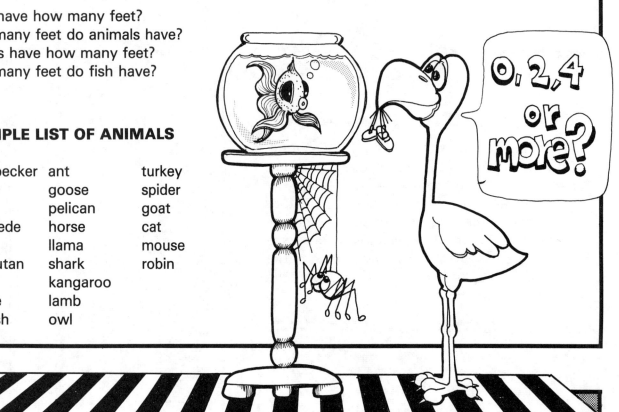

SAMPLE LIST OF ANIMALS

woodpecker	ant	turkey
wolf	goose	spider
whale	pelican	goat
centipede	horse	cat
eagle	llama	mouse
orangutan	shark	robin
gorilla	kangaroo	
gazelle	lamb	
goldfish	owl	

NOISY FEET

Have students close their eyes while one student makes a sound using only his feet. Students open eyes and try to describe the sound they heard. Encourage students to verbalize what they hear.

Examples: scuffle, shuffle, tap, dance, hop, gallop, jump stamp, skip, run

A combination of two foot sounds can be made also. Children listen for pattern of sounds.

Examples: two taps, three hops, one scuffle, three stomps

STARTING OUT ON THE RIGHT FOOT

Preparation:
Make several footprints and attach to the bulletin board. Attach proper lettering. Mount the classes' good work papers on the footprints, or for the New Year have the class write New Year's resolutions and mount them on the footprints. Be sure to use the "right" footprint.

Use this bulletin board at the beginning of the school year or to start out the New Year in January!

EDIBLE PEANUT BUTTER PLAY DOUGH
(1 serving)

1 tbs. peanut butter
1 tbs. honey
1 tbs. powdered milk
Mix all together to make dough.

Use to make letters of the alphabet and words.

Spell names of children's family members and lay the letters across plates as "name cards."

BAREFOOT MARBLE RACE

Tell the class to remove their shoes and socks. Place two marbles on the starting line in front of each team. On signal, the first child in each line grasps a marble with the toes of each foot and walks to the finish line. If he drops a marble, he must pick it up with his toes before continuing.

TYING SHOES RELAY

Each team member must have on shoes that have ties. First person on each team is handed a pair of gloves. They must tie their shoe strings with the gloves on before handing the gloves to the next team member.

DUTCH-SHOE RELAY

Provide each relay team with two shoe boxes. On signal, each player in turn places his feet in the boxes and shuffles up to the goal line and back to starting point where the change takes place.

SCIENCE CHALLENGE

Challenge the class with this question: Can you do two things at the same time? Most people cannot. Have each child print his name on a piece of paper, then move his foot in a circle. Try to do both at the same time. Ask why it is hard to do. The reason is because he has to think about his hand and foot doing different things.

SCIENCE QUESTION

Which Is Longer?

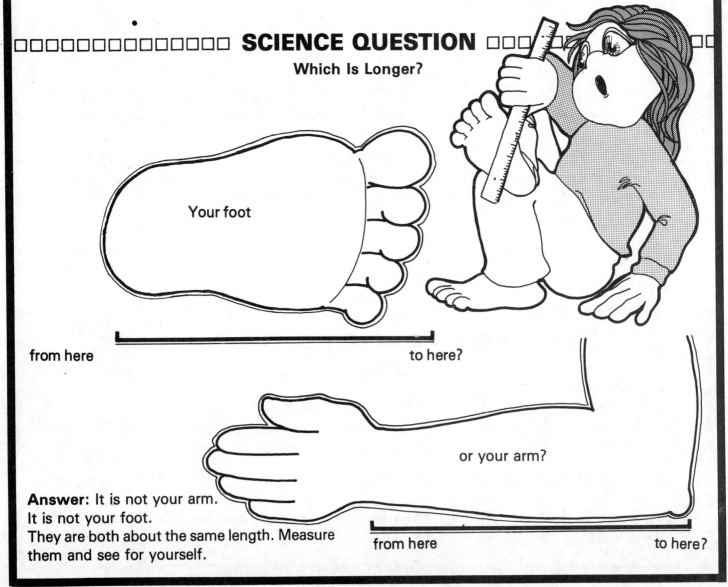

Your foot

from here   to here?

or your arm?

Answer: It is not your arm.
It is not your foot.
They are both about the same length. Measure them and see for yourself.

from here   to here?

WHAT DO SHOES TELL ABOUT PEOPLE?

For Class Discussion:

Did you ever look at the shoes on people and think about how much you could know about the person who wore them? There are the high brown, muddy, ditchdiggers' shoes, or the shining patent leather little girl's dress shoes. There are the little boy's cowboy boots, well worn and run down at the heels, or mother's high heeled dress shoes. When you look at a shoe, immediately it brings a story to your mind. If you think about it long enough, you will know if the wearer was old or young, neat or sloppy, man or woman, kind of occupation, on his feet a lot, etc.

Look at your shoes. What do they tell about you?

Give each child a copy of a boot or let each one draw a shoe of his own. On the shoe or boot, have each child write what his shoe tells about himself. Have these shoes or boots walk around your classroom walls.

Shoe Adjectives

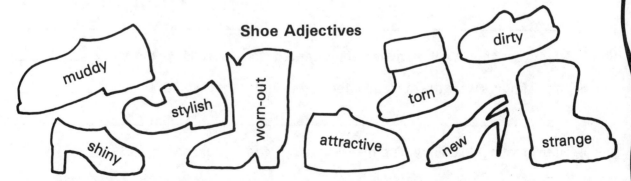

Select a shoe adjective and write sentences telling about people in different walks of life by the shoes they wear.

PANTOMIME

Have the children pantomime to the following:

How I'd walk if . . .
1. There was a nail in my shoe.
2. I was walking on a muddy road in my best shoes.
3. I was walking on one ski.

How I'd accomplish the following if . . .
4. My hands were tied behind my back and my nose itched.
5. I had a cast on one hand and I needed to put on my coat and button it.
6. I had mud on both my hands and was asked to zip up my friend's coat.

THE DANCE OF THE GLOVES

Divide the class into four or five groups. One group at a time puts on gloves, any kind, and each member moves his hands in time to music. Have each group practice a set routine before performing in front of the class. Use any music. *The Nutcracker Suite* would be a good choice.

SHARING TIME

Assign a sentence to be finished for a sharing time in class. Give children time to think this through and then share it in class.

1. If my feet could talk, they would say _____
   _____.

2. If my feet could walk anywhere they wanted, they would take me to _____.

3. If my fingers were the most talented in the world, they would _____
   _____.

4. If my feet could do anything they wanted to, they would choose to _____
   _____.

5. If my toes could have a personality, they'd choose that of _____.

BOOT GARDEN

Bright pretty flowers look cheery in an old boot, an old worn-out tennis shoe, or an old roller skate.

Put a little gravel in the bottom of the boot and fill it with damp potting soil. Plant a few flower seeds or a cactus in the soil. This makes a simple and unusual planter from a recycled item, and your planter will also become a terrific conversation piece.

MAKING BOOKS

MAKING BOOKS

The Snowy Day, by Ezra Jack Keats, and *Big Tracks, Little Tracks*, by Franklyn M. Branley, are two books with "tracks" (footprints) as themes.

Expand this theme . . . spy prints, mystery footprints, paw marks, the invisible trail. Allow the children to trace their own footprints for the cover and shape of this book. Have them create their own stories on "tracks."

MUDDY HAND COOKIES

⅔ cup butter
1 cup sugar
2 tsp. vanilla
2 eggs
2½ cups flour
½ cup unsweetened cocoa mix
½ tsp. baking soda
¼ tsp. salt

Cream butter, sugar and vanilla together. Add eggs and mix well. Add dry ingredients, blending thoroughly. Chill dough until firm. Roll dough out to ¼ inch thick. Lay your hand on the dough and cut around it to make your handprint. Bake on an ungreased sheet at 350° for 6—8 minutes.

ABC "MUD" COOKIES

These cookies spell words. The letters are shaped from a special "mud" dough that handles like modeling clay. Make enough dough for everyone to spell his or her name.

4 ½ cups unsifted flour
½ cup cocoa mix
1 ½ cups butter
3 hard-cooked egg yolks
¾ cup sugar
3 raw egg yolks
1 ½ tsp. vanilla

To make the dough, measure flour into a bowl and add cocoa mix. Add butter and cut into small pieces. Mix mud mixture with your clean fingers until the flour mixture and butter form fine crumbs. Mash hard-cooked egg yolks with sugar and stir into the flour mixture. Blend raw egg yolks with vanilla and stir into the flour mixture with a fork.

Press the mud mixture with your hands into a firm ball. Keep the ball covered. Work with the dough at room temperature but refrigerate it if you make it ahead.

Roll out the dough. Cut three or four-inch strips that you can roll between your palms to make ropes. Shape the ropes into letters. Flatten them slightly so they're about ¼ inch thick. Bake 25 minutes in a 300° oven.

FINGER PAINT
(Quick Method)

Dampen the table with a wet sponge to prevent the paper from slipping. Wet the paper with the sponge, too.

Pour liquid starch on top of the slick paper or shelf paper and add powdered tempera or food coloring to color.

Have your students make different patterns on their papers.

CREATE A SCULPTURE YOU CAN EAT

Here's a fun way to create edible sculptures or shellac them to preserve them as decorations!

Sprinkle 1 package of dry yeast into 1½ cups of very warm water. Stir until the yeast is dissolved.

Mix in 1 egg, ¼ cup honey, ¼ cup shortening, and 1 teaspoon salt.

Stir in 5 cups of flour, a little at a time, until you have a ball of dough that's not too sticky to handle. Knead the dough 5 minutes on waxed paper.

On a cookie sheet, have the children shape the dough into flat figures.

Cover the sculptures with a towel and let them rise in a warm place for 25 minutes. Let them rise longer if you want them fatter.

Bake at 350° about 20 minutes or until golden brown.

The children can eat their creations or shellac them when they are cool.

FOOT PATHS

Here is an activity for kindergarten children designed to teach and reinforce colors and coordination.

Cut a sheet of paper approximately twenty feet long. Cut many footprints from the eight basic colors using construction paper, or have the children trace and cut out their own footprints to use. Glue the footprints on the paper so that there is a path of four colors. Later change and use four different colors. The children walk the path staying on a particular color.

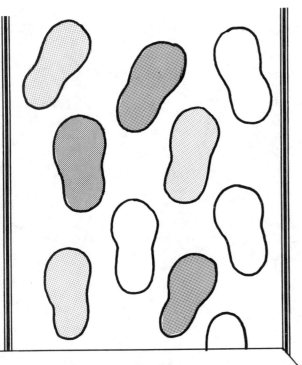

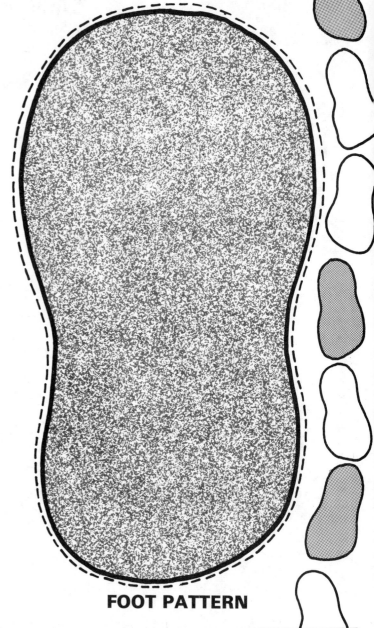

FOOT PATTERN

CREPE PAPER CLAY

You will need:
1 ½ cups torn crepe paper pieces
1 ½ cups water
½ cup flour

Let the torn paper soak in water overnight. Then drain off the water and mix in the flour. Knead like dough. Mold the mixture into shapes. Have the children try shaping it like their footprints or handprints.

POPCORN FUN ON A RAINY DAY

There's always something warm and comforting about eating freshly popped corn with others, especially when it is raining outside. Popcorn will quickly create an atmosphere of fun in your classroom. It is inexpensive, healthful, and always a favorite. You will find many eager learners when popcorn is used as a teaching tool.

Inside this popcorn I have drawn my favorite person to share popcorn with.

Here is a picture of my favorite place to munch popcorn.

Here are my favorite things to put on popcorn.

This is a picture of my favorite drink to have with popcorn.

Have the class write a story about how it would feel to be a kernel of popcorn that gets popped. Ask them to include dialogue. If the kernels could talk . . . what would they say?

POPCORN VERBS

poured

munch

ate

crunched

popped

Select popcorn verbs and write sentences having to do with popcorn on a rainy day.

HISTORY OF POPCORN

To the Teacher: Share with your class some history of popcorn.

Popcorn was already well-known to the Indians when the white man arrived in America. In New Mexico archeologists found some popped corn in a bat cave. It was thought to be over five thousand years old. Indians of North America popped corn and ate it as food, used it as a decoration and in religious ceremonies. An Indian brought an offering of popped corn for the first Thanksgiving celebration, but long before that the Incas were growing this unique exploding corn. Pottery corn poppers have been found in excavations in Peru. They are remarkably similar to a modern skillet with a lid.

Governor Bradford of Plymouth described it as corn that turned itself inside out and was all white and fluffy. But the Plymouth children did not have butter to season their popcorn because there were no cows in America for a long time.

Today the United States grows nearly all the world's popcorn. Nebraska and Indiana lead the states in popcorn production. Popcorn is as easy to grow as sweet corn in a home garden but it needs lots of rain to make it grow. Americans have chewed and crunched and enjoyed popcorn since the days of early America.

POPCORN TOSS

Label large buckets or containers (old milk jugs or ice-cream cartons) with the numbers 1, 5, and 10. Put tape along the tops of the containers so the children will not cut themselves. Place the buckets in a vertical line in progression from small numbers to large. The children then stand on a designated line and toss leftover popcorn kernels into the containers. They then add up their scores of the buckets they got the popcorn into or play this as a team game with two teams and see which team can get the most points.

THE POPCORN OLYMPICS

Have the children pretend they just entered the Popcorn Olympics. Tell about the event each one entered, the course, how the competition was held and who won. Have them write three to five paragraphs about their experience in the Popcorn Olympics.

POPCORN MONSTER BAG

You discover a popcorn monster in your classroom closet. The monster offers you a bag of treasures in trade for a bowl of popcorn you are eating. Will you trade?

Write your answer inside the popcorn monster bag and tell why you would or would not trade. If you choose the treasures, then tell about the treasures you expect to receive.

Activity: Popcorn Game

Have the children make a popcorn word search or crossword puzzle.

PIP POP POPCORN

Words and Music by Chuck Hardy

Pip pop pop up some pop—corn when its too wet to run out and play slip, slop, siz-zle the but—ter on a drip drop driz-zly day this o—rig-i-nal re-ci-pe straight from the ker-nel ex—plodes in-to a puff when heat-ed red hot in-ter-nal; so just shake,shake,shake,shake shake on the salt, Cre-ate some cra-zy corn in a nat-u-ral way, and pop some fun in-to a rain-y day.

POPCORN TREE

Pop some popcorn. The fun of this project is that children can eat while they create!

Give each child a piece of blue paper. Have him use a brown crayon to draw a tree with many branches, and then glue the popcorn on the tree branches to make snow for winter or blossoms for spring.

Have the children draw either snow scenes around their trees with chalk for winter or spring scenes around their trees with crayons. They can eat what popcorn is left over!

POPCORN LEGENDS

No one knows where this mysterious plant started its journey, but popcorn was thought to be discovered by Indians thousands of years ago. The Indians had a legend about popcorn. They said that inside each kernel of popcorn lived a little demon. The demon would get so mad when his house was heated up that he exploded.

Have the students make up other stories about why popcorn pops. Allow time for them to share their stories.

Explain to the class that when popcorn kernels are heated, the moisture turns into steam. The steam builds up pressure within the shell, eventually causing the kernel to burst and the inside to puff out. The kernels expand thirty to forty times their original size when popped.

SCIENCE ON THE FLOOR

Divide the class into four teams. Give each team a bowl of popcorn. Name something they are studying in science or social studies and have each team try to create that picture on the floor. If you want to keep their pictures, have them do this on mural paper and use glue with the popcorn. You might like to have the teams do four different pictures and, when they are dry, mount on the classroom wall.

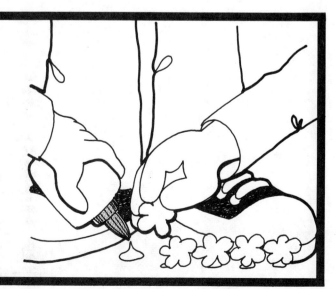

A GUESSING GAME

Each day for a week or two, place fifty to one hundred kernels of popped corn in a plastic bag. As the children get ready to leave for the day, let each child guess the number of popped kernels in the bag. After everyone has had a guess, count the kernels as a class project. Everyone can count along. The one that guesses the nearest to the actual number gets to take the bag of popcorn to munch on the way home.

CRUNCHY POPCORN FRUIT MUNCH

3 quarts popped popcorn
2 cups natural cereal with raisins
¾ cup dried apricots, chopped
¼ tsp. salt
½ cup butter
½ cup honey

Combine popcorn, cereal, apricots, and salt in a large baking pan. In a small saucepan, combine butter and honey. Cook over low heat until butter is melted. Pour over popcorn mixture, tossing lightly until well-coated. Place in oven at 300° for 30 minutes, stirring occasionally. Makes 3 quarts. Store in tightly covered container.

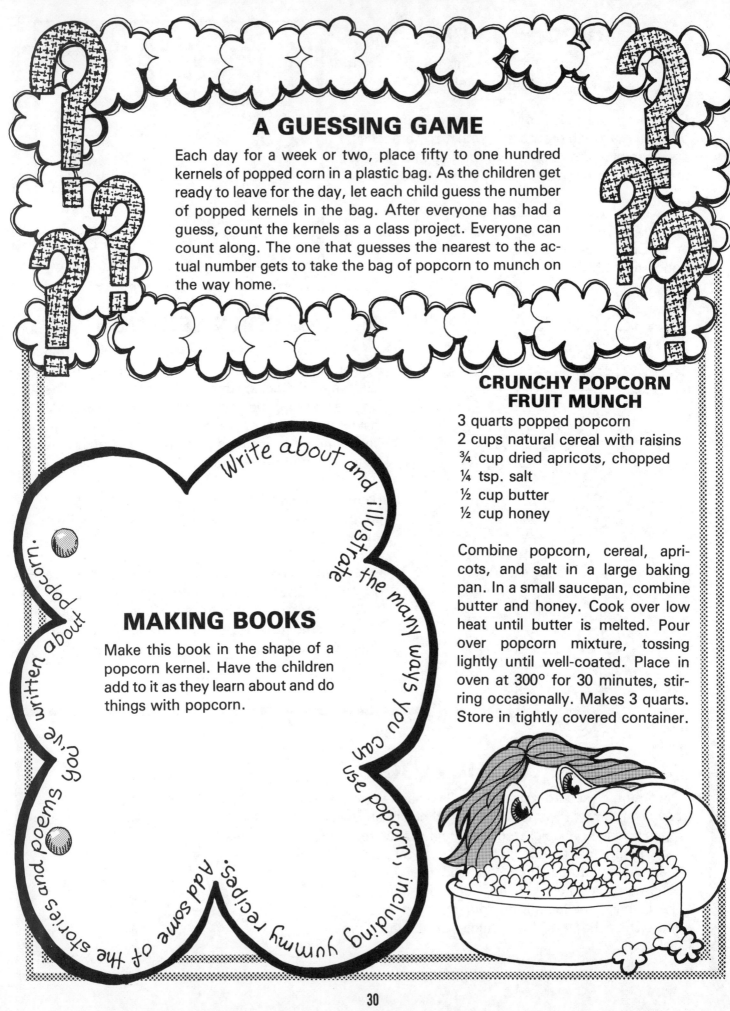

Write about and illustrate the many ways you can use popcorn, including yummy recipes. Add some of the stories and poems you've written about popcorn.

MAKING BOOKS

Make this book in the shape of a popcorn kernel. Have the children add to it as they learn about and do things with popcorn.

THE POPCORN DRAGON

Pop a big batch of popcorn and put it in small paper bags. While the class is outside, hide the bags of popcorn around the room. When the children return, instruct them to use their noses to track down the popcorn. When each child has found a bag, make a circle and get ready for a popcorn story.

Read to the class *The Popcorn Dragon,* by Jane Thayer. Allow plenty of time for questions and answers after the story. Suggested questions:

1. How did the dragon feel when he discovered he could blow smoke?
2. How did the animals feel when they saw Dexter blowing smoke?
3. Have you ever heard someone brag? How did it make you feel?
4. Have you ever learned something new and wanted to share it with your friends?
5. What is the difference between sharing and bragging?

If time allows, choose a Dexter, an elephant, a zebra, and a giraffe. Let them reenact the story using their own dialogue.

I'm Snow Puff!

PICK A NAME

There are many kinds of popcorn. They are white hull-less, yellow hull-less, red kernels, calico, and even black popcorn, but they all pop white. "Dynamite" and "Snow Puff" are the biggest kernels. Ask the children to think of a new name for popcorn that pops as big as apples. List the ideas on the chalkboard. Vote and choose the favorite name. Encourage the children to write stories about this new popcorn.

Just call me Dynamite!

ACTIVITIES

The following are popcorn-related activities you can use to motivate your students:
1. List as many things as you can about popcorn.
2. List what other things you can think of that are light, white, and fluffy.
3. Make a list of things you could do with popcorn.
4. Make a one-minute speech on "Why popcorn is . . . ."

Have the students be creative in the following activities.
1. Design some popcorn stationery.
2. Pretend you are "Dynamite" popcorn and write a story about how you became "Dynamite" popcorn.
3. Read some classic myths or *Just So Stories.* Make up your own story to explain "How the Popcorn Got Its Pop."
4. Make up a popcorn game. Design a gameboard using questions about social studies or math.
5. What kind of a design can you dream up for a popcorn T-shirt? Draw your idea and don't forget that a T-shirt has both a front and a back.
6. Suppose one rainy afternoon you were about to eat some popcorn. All of a sudden it could talk. List five questions you would ask it. List another five questions it would ask you.
7. Write a poem about popcorn.
8. See how many words you can make out of *Popcorn Tastes Great!* Using those words, create a story with popcorn as the theme.

POPCORN PARTY MIX

2 quarts popped popcorn
2 cups slim pretzel sticks
2 cups cheese curls
¼ cup butter
1 tbs. Worcestershire sauce
½ tsp. garlic salt
½ tsp. seasoned salt

In a shallow baking pan, mix popcorn, pretzel sticks and cheese curls. Melt butter in small saucepan and stir in seasonings. Pour over dry mixture and mix well. Bake at 250° for 45 minutes, stirring several times. Makes 2½ quarts.

MARSHMALLOW-CHOCOLATE POPCORN BALLS

5 quarts popped popcorn
1 7-oz. jar marshmallow topping
1 12-oz. package chocolate chips
2 tbs. water
1 tsp. vanilla

Place popped corn in large greased pan. Melt marshmallow topping and chocolate chips in top of double boiler. Stir in water and vanilla. Pour chocolate mixture over popcorn. Shape quickly into balls with buttered hands. You can create animals or your own creatures. Makes about 14.

Preparation:

Using 9″ x 12″ pieces of colored construction paper, make a rainbow on one of your bulletin boards. Each sheet of construction paper shows a space for a book report. The challenge to the entire class is to fill the rainbow with book reports. Attach proper lettering. When the rainbow is full, a treat will be found in the pot at the end of the rainbow—a popcorn party!

Other Bulletin Board Ideas

1. Cut out of white construction paper large kernels of popcorn and attach them to the bulletin board. Show off any of the activities done in this section, such as popcorn puzzles or word searches, popcorn stories, popcorn trees, popcorn monster bags, etc., by mounting them on the popcorn kernels. Attach the lettering: ''Popping Good.''

2. To display good work papers, mount them on the popcorn kernels and label this bulletin board: ''Popping with Top Scores.'' You could even have a corn popper in the lower center of the bulletin board with the popcorn popping out.

POPCORN PUPPETS

Pop a huge bowlful of popcorn so the children have plenty to eat as they string. Let the popcorn sit for a day or two to soften; it will be less likely to break. Do not butter it, but salt is okay.

String the popcorn on thin wire. Cut lengths of six or eight inches for arms and legs and about ten inches for body and head. Poke the wire through a soft part of each kernel close to the middle. Remind the children to be careful not to prick their fingers on the sharp ends of the wire.

When the body wire is full, bend one end into a loop for a head. Twist the end of the wire around the neck. Arms and legs are single strands, bent in the middle. Twist the arms around the neck. Bend the bottom end of the body wire around the center of the leg strand. Gently bend the arms and legs to look like lively puppets. Attach string and hang from ceiling lights.

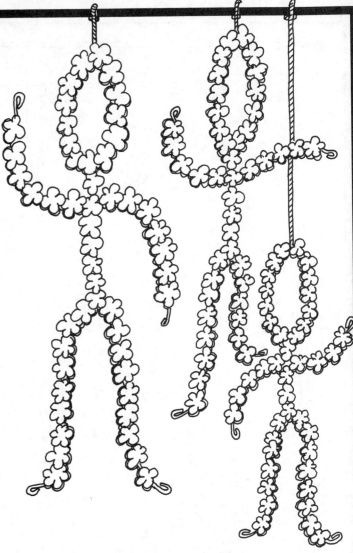

POPCORN CAKE

1 ¼ cups unpopped yellow popcorn
½ cup melted butter
⅓ cup oil
1 bag small marshmallows
1 13-oz. can mixed nuts or peanuts
2 cups small gumdrops

Pop the popcorn and put it in a large container. Mix together the butter, oil, and marshmallows. Add nuts and gumdrops to the popcorn. Pour the butter mixture over all. Press the mixture into a buttered angel cake tin. Cool and let harden until crisp. Refrigerate. Makes a delicious popcorn cake for a rainy day!

MATH TIME

Everyone enjoys eating popcorn, but the preparation can be made into a learning activity. Let the children measure the oil and popcorn and pour into the popper. Then when it is popped, measure it again and compare the difference. Weigh the kernels before and after they are popped. Do they weigh more or less? This is a good time to talk about volume and expansion, weight, etc.

The children could count the kernels that popped and compare with the number that did not pop. This could lead to a discussion on ratios, etc., for the older children. Using leftover popcorn, try several activities to incorporate math concepts into the learning process. Have the class make up story problems using the popcorn. Reinforce counting concepts for younger children. Have them write the number word for the groups of popcorn.

POPCORN PICTURES

Provide a popcorn center in your classroom. Have available on a table a large bowl of popcorn, various colors of construction paper, glue, scissors, and other art materials. Allow each child time at the popcorn center to create his own popcorn picture. Watch children's ideas begin to pop!

A "SENSE"-ATIONAL POPCORN PARTY

A small unit on senses using popcorn

As the children return from recess, have a hidden popcorn popper popping.

Discuss what **sounds** they hear and what **smells** they smell. Prepare ahead other sounds to have the children listen to and discuss how the sounds are different. Also, have several other items for the children to smell and talk about how they are alike and how they are different.

Next have a tray or bags of items ready to **touch.** Be sure one of those items is popcorn kernels. Discuss how different objects feel different and that we can identify objects by the way they feel.

Now bring out the popcorn popper so everyone can **see** the popcorn and **taste** it. Talk about texture, color, and flavor. You could have other items for the class to taste so that they can compare salty popcorn to items that are sweet, sour, bitter, crispy, bland, etc.

POPCORN CORSAGE

Make up lots of popcorn. You might try coloring it with food coloring so many colors are available to choose from for the corsages. Precut three-inch cardboard circles for each child or cut cardboard in flower designs.

Glue popcorn to the cardboard. Have them create designs or flower shapes. Glue a green pipe cleaner to the bottom of the circle, near the edge, and curl it around like a plant stem. Let the glue dry thoroughly.

Use corsages at Thanksgiving or possibly for mothers when you have finished this unit on popcorn and have a room party with popcorn displays or let children wear them in their own buttonholes.

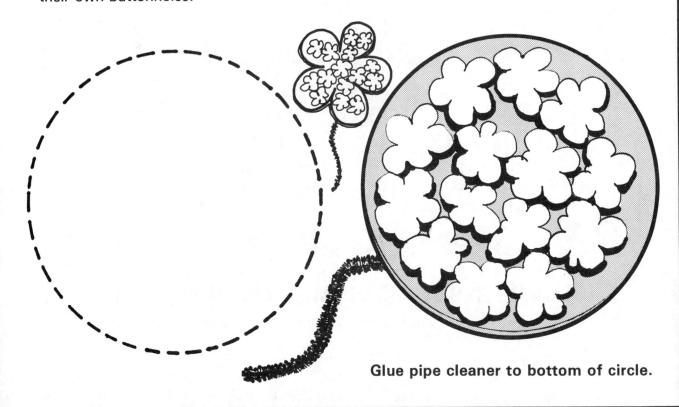

Glue pipe cleaner to bottom of circle.

PEANUT BUTTER POPCORN

8—10 cups of popped popcorn
1 cup sugar
1 cup brown sugar
1½ cups corn syrup
¼ cup butter
1½ cups peanut butter

In a saucepan, mix the sugars and corn syrup over medium heat. When the mixture starts to boil hard then boil for one minute. Remove from heat and stir in the butter and peanut butter. When the mixture is smooth, drizzle it over the popped corn, tossing and turning until the coating starts to firm up. A delight to eat in rainy weather!

36

HATS OFF TO RAINY DAYS

What can be more fun than to celebrate rainy days with a unit on hats? The children will enjoy collecting all kinds of hats and learning what hats can tell them about people's lives. They will have fun as they dive into ''Hats Off to . . .'' careers, book reports, games, puppets, difficult words, making books, recipes, synonyms, and creative writing.

Have students collect a variety of hats for the classroom ''hatbox.''

HATS OFF TO CAREERS!

Explain to your class that a hat can tell what job a person has. Discuss that not only a hat tells what job a person holds, but some hats are used for protection, for camouflage, as part of a uniform, as a decoration to fit in with the fashions or customs of the time, as an important part in displaying good manners, and some just for fun.

Discuss some of the jobs or careers represented in your hatbox, pointing out the function of some of the hats.

Let the children try on the hats and role-play the various careers the hats signify. The class might like to put on a ''Hats Off to Careers!'' presentation for another class.

HATS OFF TO A PARADE

Have a hat parade. Invite a class to come see your parade or do it for Open House. If you haven't collected enough hats, then make some as an art project. Use paper plates, construction paper, crepe paper and any items for decoration.

CLOWN HATS

Using an 18" x 24" piece of paper, cut a pattern following directions in the figure at the right. Have the children color the curved border with several colors and make many different colored polka-dots on the hat. Using strips of crepe paper, make a tassel and staple at peak of clown hat after stapling the base to fit child's head.

BASIC HAT PATTERNS

A large paper plate becomes the brim of any of the hats. Make the crowns of the hats with construction paper.

Draw the crown twice and cut it out. Glue the two crowns together, but don't glue tabs together. Spread tabs apart and glue them onto the paper plate brim. Make holes on brim near the crown to tie two yarn pieces that will tie under the child's chin to hold on the hat. Decorate hats appropriately.

INDIAN HEADDRESS

Make a band of corrugated cardboard to fit around the child's head, with corrugations running up and down. Insert feather stems into corrugation. Or draw and color feathers and glue them on the corrugation.

HATS OFF TO CAREERS MOBILE

Divide class into five groups. Give each group two hats from the hatbox representing different careers, and each group draws the rest of the body to construct these mobiles. Hang them up in the classroom.

HATS OF THE FUTURE

Have the class design Hats of the Future. Have them explain who would wear their hats. What new careers can they create with just hats?

HATS OFF TO SYNONYMS

HATSTORM!

As a class make a list of synonyms for the word *hat* or types of hats. The list might include:

derby	beret	top hat
cap	strawhat	forest ranger's hat
sunbonnet	stovepipe hat	baseball cap
nurse's hat	beanie	Panama hat
yarmulke	stocking cap	dunce cap
mortarboard	soldier's hat	nightcap
hood	coonskin cap	bowler
chapeau	skull cap	tam-o'-shanter
visor	fireman's hat	helmet
hard hat	tiara	Indian headdress
turban	habit	tricornered hat
fez	tam	halo
crown	beaver	cowboy hat
sailor's hat	policeman's hat	sombrero
bathing cap	bearskin hat	ten-gallon hat

HATS OFF TO GAMES

MUSICAL HAT GAME

Have the children sit in a circle with a cardboard box containing old clothes, etc., in it. As the music starts (teacher can use a record or play the piano), an old hat is passed from head to head. When the music stops, the player wearing the hat must jump up and put on as many clothes from the box as he can before the music starts again. The winner is the player who puts on the most clothes while keeping the hat on his head.

HATS AWAY GAME

Have the children stand in a circle. Give each child a hat to place on his head. Tell the players to place their left hands behind them. On the command "Ready, change!" each one grabs the hat from the one at his right with his right hand and places it on his own head. Repeat the command and just when the group gets fairly good at it, change hands, or have them take the hat from the player at the left or put the hat from their own head on the neighboring player's head.

SKIT

Have two or three hat-wearing students write a short interaction skit based on who they are while wearing the hat.

For example: "Hats Off to Lincoln and Washington . . ."

Many books have been written about these two great leaders and provide background for dramatizing the important events of their lifetimes. Use or make a tall hat for Lincoln and a tricornered hat for Washington.

Flippy Floppy Hat

Words and Music by Chuck Hardy

Drip drop drip, drop drip drop drip drip drop I'm a
flip-py flop-py hat in a drip-py drop-py storm. And I must try to keep folks dry and
fuz-zy wuz-zy warm. When I grow up I'm going to be a brown un-brell-a wait and see, But
now I am a flip-py flop-py drip-py drop-py hat. How a-bout that! Drip, drop.

HATS OFF TO BOOK REPORTS

For oral book reports have each student pretend he is a character in the story. With a hat and a few props, have the child summarize the type of character he represents from his book. The assignment could be to read only books about hats. Hat books could include:

The 500 Hats of Bartholomew Cubbins
by Dr. Seuss
The Vanguard Press, New York, 1938

Belinda's New Spring Hat
by Eleanor Clymer
Franklin Watts, Inc., New York, 1969

Anthony's Hat
by Deborah Robison
Scholastic Book Services, New York, 1976

Jeannie's Hat
by Ezra Jack Keats
Harper & Row, New York, 1966

The Wishing Hat
By Annegert Fuchshuber
Wm. Morrow & Co., New York, 1977

Grandmother Lucy & Her Hats
by Joyce Wood
Atheneum, New York, 1969

Another idea for book reports would be to have each student make a stick puppet, dressing it in a hat (and clothes if desired) to play the part of a favorite storybook character. Write the name of the book on the Popsicle stick. Keep the puppets in a special box on a shelf in your classroom library.

Puppet Directions:

SIMPLE STICK PUPPETS

Make simple stick puppets by attaching construction paper or cardboard cutouts to Popsicle sticks, straws, or tongue depressors. Draw on faces and glue on yarn hair and construction paper clothes (if desired). Design the hats to represent characters in the stories.

Still another idea for book reports on hats would be to have each child make a construction paper hat replica of his hat story and write a summary of the book on the paper hat along with title and author. Attach yarn to each hat and hang from ceiling lights around the classroom. Or you could mount the hats on a bulletin board and title it "Hats Off to Book Reports."

HATS OFF TO YUMMY SNACKS

PEANUT BUTTER MINI PIZZAS

Slice an English muffin in half and toast the halves. Spread peanut butter on each half and top with any of these ingredients: honey, jelly, apple or banana slices, raisins, dry cereal, bacon pieces, salami, or pepperoni. (Variations: good with ready-made pizza or spaghetti sauce and cheese plus sliced olives, tomatoes, or pepperoni.) Pop under the broiler, or eat as is.

Yummy on a rainy day after a classroom Hat Parade or the day you present Hats Off to Careers!

Serve peanut butter mini pizzas with orange fizz, or if your students are really crazy about peanut butter, then try peanut butter milk shakes.

PEANUT BUTTER MILK SHAKE

Combine ⅓ cup milk and 3 tbs. peanut butter in a blender and blend until smooth. Add 2 cups vanilla ice cream and blend.

Pour your delicious milk shake into a glass. Makes 1 serving.

(Try adding a banana, berries, or peaches to vanilla ice cream and milk for a special flavored milk shake other than peanut butter.

ORANGE FIZZ

Combine 1 6-oz. can orange juice concentrate, 1 cup milk, 1 tsp. vanilla, 1 cup water, ½ cup sugar and 12 ice cubes in a blender.

Mix at high speed for 30 seconds.

Pour into glasses and serve cold. Makes 5 glasses of orange fizz.

Delicious and nutritious!

Preparation:

Attach various large hats made from construction paper to the bulletin board. Attach appropriate lettering.

Mount the students' good writing papers or poems about hats onto the colorful hats.

HATS OFF TO ADVERBS

Divide the class into groups. Have each group demonstrate an adverb by doing the following: walking, talking, singing, eating, dancing.

Now have each group pantomime the following adverbs in sentences and see if the other students can figure out the sentences.

MAKING BOOKS

Have each child pretend he is a magical hat. What magic can you do? Do you make people happy or sad with your magic? Do you travel to different lands? To whom do you belong? What people do you meet with your magic ways? Choose a title for your book and draw a picture for the cover to match your magical hat in the story.

Read *Frosty the Snowman* to the class.

HATS OFF TO DIFFICULT WORDS!

Children can learn by listening, writing, imagery and touch. In using imagery and writing, have the children select words from their spelling lesson they feel they need to learn. Using colored pencils, they can create pictures by writing the words over and over in lines to form the shapes of various objects. Mount their pictures on colored paper made in various hat shapes to display on the bulletin board. You could title the bulletin board "Hats Off to Difficult Words!"

Variation of this would be to shape your object to match the word, such as the word *fish.*

HATS OFF TO HATS

Use the hats listed in "Hatstorm," page 39, and the following clues to work the puzzle.

Down:
1. A flat, round cap
2. Worn in sports or by knights
4. An academic cap with a square, flat top
9. A covering for the head and neck

Across:
3. A skullcap worn by Jewish men
5. A Scottish cap with a flat circular top
6. A woman's crownlike headdress of jewels or flowers
7. *Hat* in French
8. A derby hat
10. A broad-brimmed hat worn in Mexico

Have the students make up their own crossword puzzles using types of hats and the dictionary. Have them exchange puzzles and work them.

Make up a classroom book of hat crosswords to keep in your library.

CREATIVE WRITING

Write a story about "The Parade of Hats." Include in the story: Who's the leader? Where's the parade? What's the occasion? When is the parade? Who will come to it? How do the hats feel being in a parade?

_____

_____

_____

_____

_____

_____

_____

_____

HATS THAT ADVERTISE

Many times hats are used for advertising. Show and discuss with your class some examples of this type of advertising.

Then give each student construction paper, scissors, glue and other art materials and have him create a hat to advertise a product.

Hang your hats from the ceiling lights or put them on a bulletin board labeled, "Hats That Advertise."

Another idea is to have them put on their own "thinking caps" and have each one create a hat to advertise a product that you know does not presently have a hat to advertise it.

FLIPPY FLOPPY HAT DRAWINGS

After learning the song in this unit on page 41, have your class draw pictures of what the flippy, floppy, drippy, droppy hat looks like to them.

You could also let them make construction paper creations of the flippy floppy hat and wear their hats when they sing the song. If you decide to put on a hat program as suggested in this unit, then this song, along with the hats, would be a cute addition to your program.

FIRE CHIEF HAT MAZE

Help the fire chief find his way to the burning house. Start at the arrow.

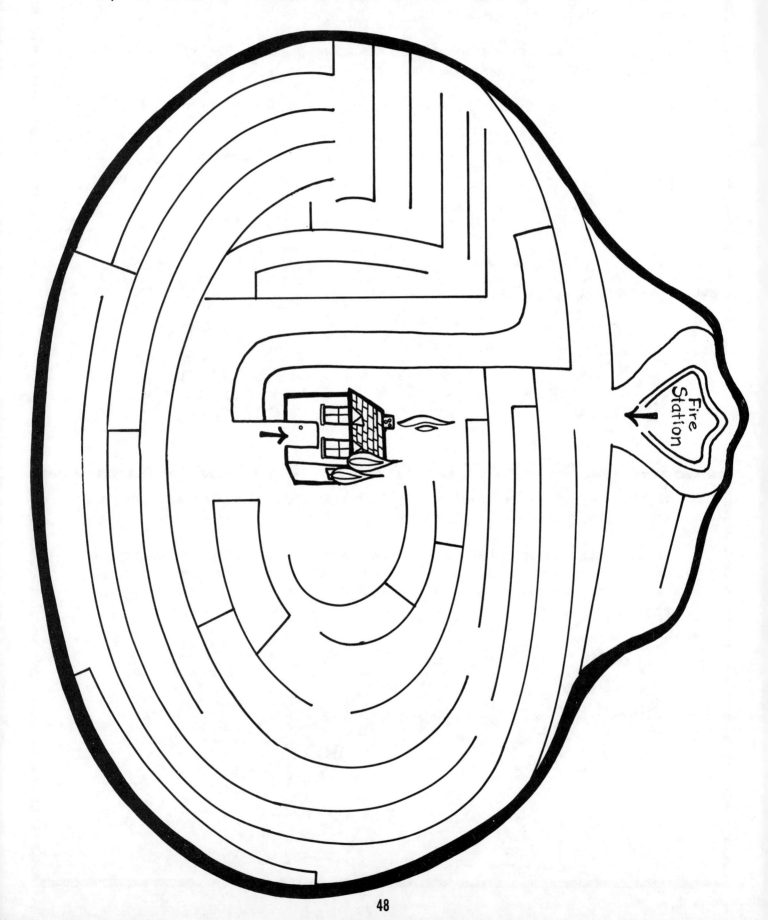

RAINDROPS AND TEARDROPS

Children need to develop a positive image of themselves and to have self-confidence. They need to discover how important they are to themselves and to others and to learn how to express their emotions. This unit will help children learn the skills of planning an activity, working on it and completing it to develop a sense of responsibility and follow-through that will promote feelings of accomplishment and pride. They will learn about themselves and to express their feelings and know that it is okay to feel that way—that each one has his own identity and is a unique person.

"ALL ABOUT ME" BOOK

Have the children put together "All About Me" books. In them they can record trips, their birthday, hobbies, family, friends, favorite games, pets, special events in their lives at home or at school. Tell them to express their feelings and to include drawings or photographs. Have them draw pictures of themselves on the fronts of their books. This project will develop a sense of importance.

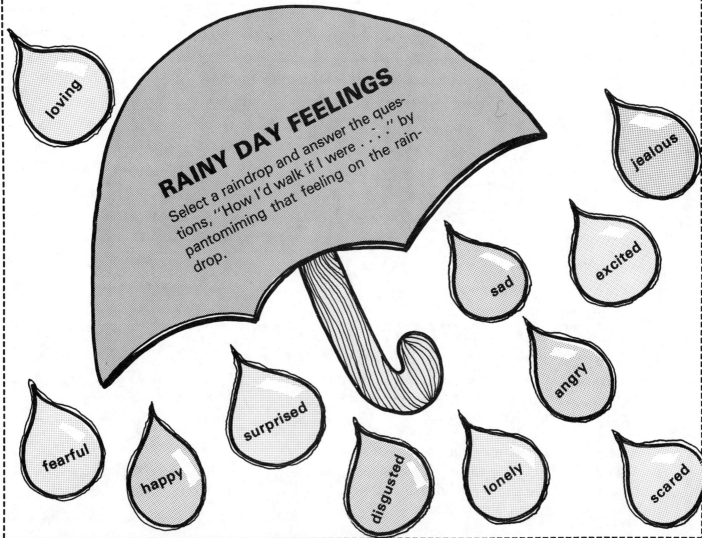

RAINY DAY FEELINGS

Select a raindrop and answer the questions, "How I'd walk if I were . . . ." by pantomiming that feeling on the raindrop.

loving · jealous · excited · sad · surprised · angry · fearful · happy · disgusted · lonely · scared

SELF-PORTRAIT

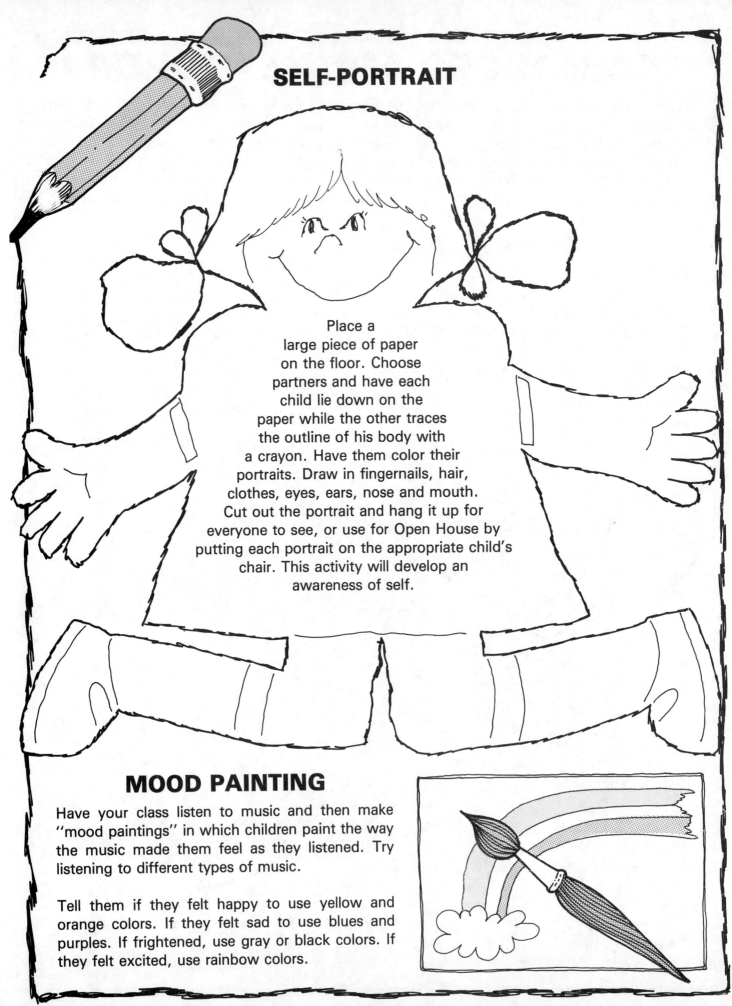

Place a large piece of paper on the floor. Choose partners and have each child lie down on the paper while the other traces the outline of his body with a crayon. Have them color their portraits. Draw in fingernails, hair, clothes, eyes, ears, nose and mouth. Cut out the portrait and hang it up for everyone to see, or use for Open House by putting each portrait on the appropriate child's chair. This activity will develop an awareness of self.

MOOD PAINTING

Have your class listen to music and then make "mood paintings" in which children paint the way the music made them feel as they listened. Try listening to different types of music.

Tell them if they felt happy to use yellow and orange colors. If they felt sad to use blues and purples. If frightened, use gray or black colors. If they felt excited, use rainbow colors.

MAKING MASKS
(Faces that tell how they feel)

Children have to learn about their feelings and the feelings of others. Since feelings are sometimes hard to pin down, making masks for different feelings will provide a chance to talk about each feeling. Be ready to accept what your students say.

Each child will need a partner. One at a time put a large paper bag over each other's head and with a pencil, carefully mark where the two eyeholes should be. Cut out holes for eyes.

Use crayons to draw the face. Small paper cups or egg carton cups attached with cellophane tape may be used for a nose. Paper strips that have been fringed or curled can be glued on for hair.

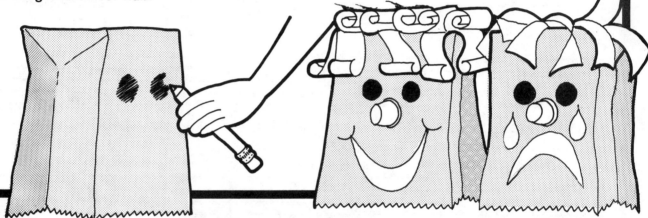

MAKING PUPPETS

Puppets are a wonderful way for children to act out their feelings, too. Here are some puppets that are easy for children to make. Have the puppets represent different feelings such as happiness, sadness, or anger.

PAPER BAG PUPPETS

Draw a face on a paper bag with crayons or felt-tip pen, or draw parts of a face on separate paper. Cut them out and glue them on the bag. Stuff the bag with crushed newspaper and put a stick or a tube from a roll of paper towels part way into the paper bag. Tie the neck with a piece of string. Glue on yarn or paper curls for hair.

SOCK PUPPETS

Stuff the toe of an old sock with a rag or cotton. Put in a stick and tie the sock with a piece of string. Put the face on with colored felt-tip pen; or sew on buttons for eyes, nose and mouth. Use yarn for hair. Be prepared to discuss feelings using the puppets.

I HAVE FEELINGS

Words and Music by Don Mitchell

Verse One

I have—feel-ings and you do too. I'd like to share a few with you.

Some-times I'm hap-py and some-times I'm sad. Some-times I'm scared, and some-times mad.

The most im-por-tant feel-ing you see, is that I'm proud of be-ing me.

Chorus

I feel just right—in the skin I wear, there's no one like me an-y-where. I

feel just right— in the skin I wear. There's no one like me an-y-where.

Verse Two: No one sees the things I see, behind my eyes is only me.
And no one knows where my feelings begin for there's only me inside my skin.
No one does what I can do, I'll be me, and you be you.
Chorus:

Verse Three: It's a wonderful thing how everyone owns just enough skin to cover his bones.
My dad's would be too big to fit, I'd be all wrinkled inside of it.
Baby sister's would be much too small, it wouldn't cover me up at all.
Chorus:

LOVE-A-GRAM

Cut out letters and words of various sizes and styles from magazines or newspapers. Arrange the letters to make phrases or sentences and glue onto a card. Try combining words or individual letters with pictures to spell out your message. Send your message to someone to cheer them up on a rainy day.

LAUGH PICTURE

Make someone laugh on a rainy day with a "laugh" picture by painting or drawing a picture you know will make that person laugh and feel happy.

TELLING HOW YOU FEEL

List some of your fears.

List what weather frightens you.

List how you feel when you cry.

List the good things in your life to help your fears disappear.

List how the sun makes you feel.

List how you feel when you laugh.

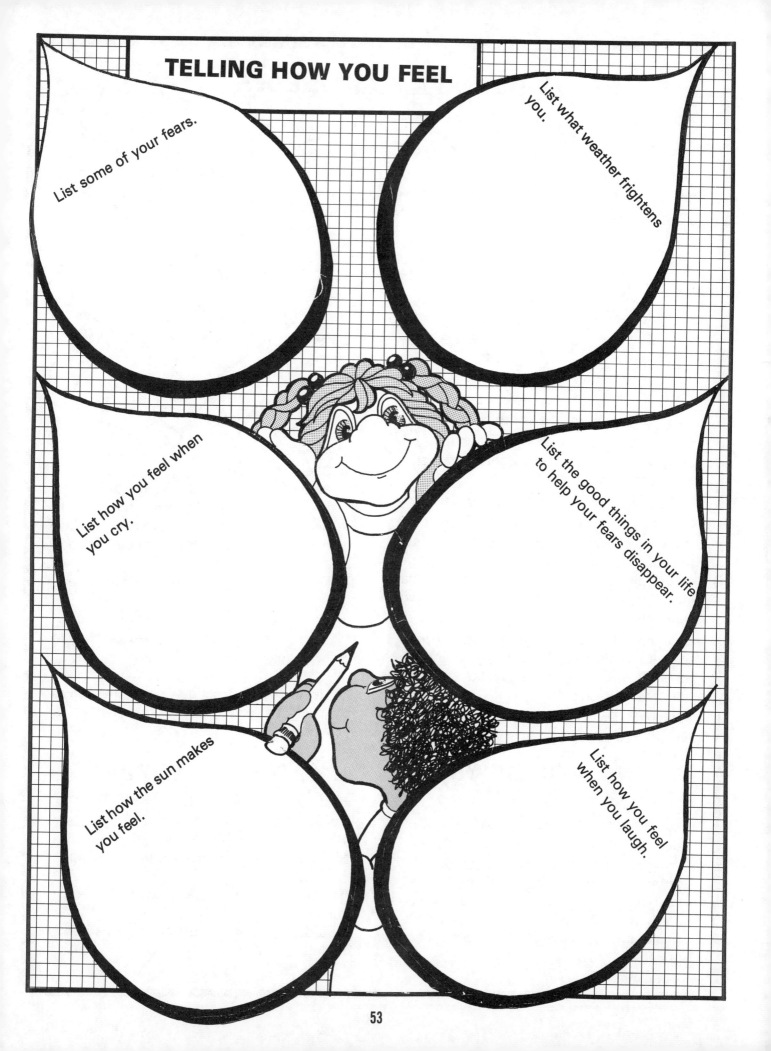

53

PATCHWORK RAINBOW

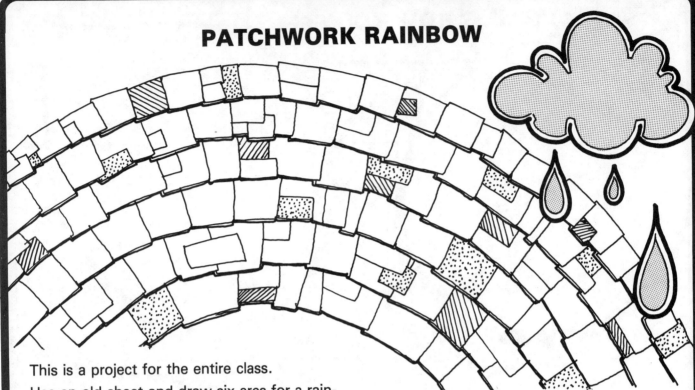

This is a project for the entire class.

Use an old sheet and draw six arcs for a rainbow. Trim away any extra sheet that isn't a part of the rainbow.

Make each arc a different color using red, orange, yellow, green, blue and purple.

Have the children cut or tear patches of fabric for each color. They can be prints, stripes, solids, plaid, etc. You might divide the class into six sections and let each section work separately on a color.

Glue the red patches on the first strip. Arrange them so that they can mix different fabric textures. Overlap the edges. Do the same with the other five colors.

Attach the class rainbow to a bulletin board or hang it in a window.

For Class Discussion:

1. Discuss the different textures of fabrics. Bring out the different textures in people—how we are all different and that it takes all kinds to make up our world.

2. Discuss how each color makes them feel.

3. Have them describe what they think of when they look at the varied patches in each color.

4. Have them describe what their lives would be like if they were rainbows of many colors.

CAN YOU DRINK RAINDROPS?

Next time it rains set an empty glass outside. Catch some raindrops in it. Raindrops are pure water. You can drink raindrops, although the water may taste strange. One percent of all the water on Earth is fresh water for us to use. It is found on the surface of the earth and under the ground.

CAN YOU BELIEVE?

Water we use every day:
Toilet flush = 5 to 7 gallons
Shower = 25 to 50 gallons
Hand washing = 2 gallons with the tap running
Tooth brushing = 2 gallons with the tap running
Outdoor watering = 5 to 10 gallons per minute

MESSAGE COOKIES

Write thirty messages that will make others feel happy on a rainy day on strips of paper and fold them.

Mix sugar into the egg whites and blend until fluffy.

Melt the butter and cool it.

To the sugar and egg white mixture, add flour, salt, vanilla, water and butter. Beat until the batter is smooth.

Grease a cookie sheet and pour batter from a spoon to form three-inch circles. Bake at 375° for eight minutes.

Place a "message" on each circle, fold it in thirds, then bend it gently in the center. If the cookies become too hard to bend, put them back in the oven for a minute.

Ingredients:
4 egg whites
1 cup sugar
½ cup melted butter
½ cup flour
¼ tsp. salt
½ tsp. vanilla
2 tbs. water

The world is a rainbow!

Lead a class discussion on how busy family members are in the home and how the children can do their part to make their home a better place to live. Here's a fun and exciting way for each child to help out in the home and make it more enjoyable with "secret handprints" left by a very special loving person.

Have each child make ten handprints and when he has helped someone secretly, he should leave one of the handprints behind.

EXPRESSING FEELINGS THROUGH CREATIVE WRITING

Have students select one of the following to write about:
1. Pretend you opened a door in your home and discovered a room you never knew was there. Describe that room and what you would do in it. How does the room make you feel?
2. Pretend you are a piece of bubble gum. What are you carried in—a sack, a pocket? How do you feel? What are your feelings about being chewed and blown up? Will you be proud to enter the largest bubble contest? Do you win?
3. If you could have three wishes, what would they be?

Challenge students' imaginations with these questions:
1. How many ways can you say "I love you"?
2. How many ways can you say "good-bye"?
3. How many ways can you laugh?

CODE GAMES

Using the following code, write "secret messages" to your friends or family. Tell them how you feel on a rainy day.

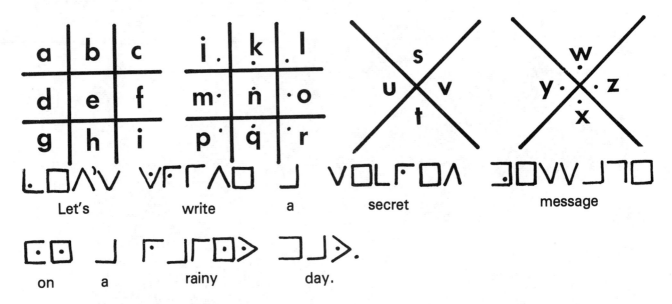

TAPE RAINY DAY SOUNDS TO CREATE POEMS

Tape the sound of rain hitting against the window or roof and write a poem about your feelings as you listen to the tape recording.

"ME" BULLETIN BOARD

Put a mirror in the center of a bulletin board. Around the mirror attach letters that read "I Am Most Important!" Have the class draw pictures of parents, grandparents, brothers, sisters, friends, etc., and attach those to the bulletin board. At the top of the board put "People Who Have Helped Make Me What I Am."

"ME" MOBILE

Have each child collect pictures and make drawings, etc., about himself. This could go from his birth to the present. The mobile could tell about friends, secrets, family, dreams, feelings, experiences, likes and dislikes, etc. Hang mobiles up in the classroom.

"CAKE" CONES

These look like ice-cream cones, but they are filled with cake.

Prepare any flavor cake mix according to the directions on the package.

Spoon cake batter into ice-cream cones with flat bottoms about 3/4 full. As a special surprise, write messages on small strips of paper, fold them and put into the batter of each one.

Set the cones in a cake pan and bake according to the package directions for cupcakes.

Prepare frosting. When the "cake" cones are cool, frost and decorate them.

Makes twelve "cake" cones.

NAME DESIGNS

Fold colored construction paper in half. Open the paper and have the children write their names on the folded line with a black crayon, pressing hard.

Close the paper and rub the back with fingernails so that the crayon comes off on the other side. Trace over all the lines so they show up.

Have children decorate their name designs using crayons or marking pens, showing how they feel today.

WHEN I GROW UP

(feelings about growing up)

Have the students pretend they have a magic looking glass and can look ten years into the future. As they develop their stories on paper, they may want to include telling how they will be different in the future, how they will look, where they will live, how they will spend their time, and what they will enjoy doing.

Have each share his story with a class partner.

Have a happy heart!

MAKING BOOKS

Make this book in the shape of one of your friends. On the shape write some characteristics of a friend.

Inside your book include pages on:
1. How many ways do you know to make or keep a friend?
2. How many ways can you make your friend smile?
3. How do you feel when a friend doesn't sit by you on the school bus?
4. How do you feel when a friend does something special for you? Do something special for your friend!
5. Write a letter to a friend expressing your feelings toward him.
6. Explain what friendship is to you.
7. What kind of a friend are you?

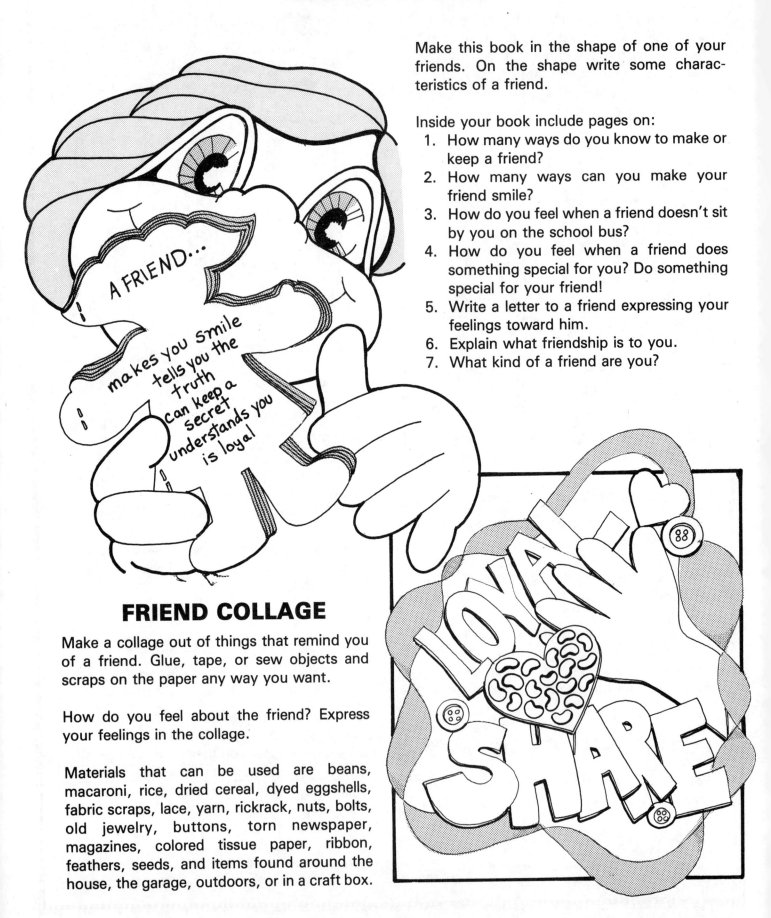

A FRIEND...
makes you smile
tells you the truth
can keep a secret
understands you
is loyal

LOYAL SHARE

FRIEND COLLAGE

Make a collage out of things that remind you of a friend. Glue, tape, or sew objects and scraps on the paper any way you want.

How do you feel about the friend? Express your feelings in the collage.

Materials that can be used are beans, macaroni, rice, dried cereal, dyed eggshells, fabric scraps, lace, yarn, rickrack, nuts, bolts, old jewelry, buttons, torn newspaper, magazines, colored tissue paper, ribbon, feathers, seeds, and items found around the house, the garage, outdoors, or in a craft box.

WHAT IS A FRIEND?

Directions for the Teacher:
To compile a class book on "What Is a Friend?" ask your class to first discuss and answer the question, "What is a friend?" This is a good opportunity for discussing feelings on friendship. Then give them pencils and white paper to draw the pictures of their answers and to include their responses and names on the papers. Encourage them to use all of the paper leaving a ½" margin on all four sides.

The pages of the booklet can be traced by you with a thin black felt-tip pen and then photocopied, making enough books for each student.

This same idea can be used with any topic and made into booklets.

59

A FRIEND IS

Words and Music by Don Mitchell

A friend is some-one you tell things to, To help you un-der-stand what you're go-ing through A friend is some-one who helps you un-der-stand What you're say-ing.

Chorus

When I tried to think of what a friend is, I thought of the way I feel a-bout you.

A friend is someone you imitate,
We imitate those we emulate.
A friend is someone you feel comfortable with,
Doing nothing with.
Chorus
A friend is someone who will defend you,
But not necessarily the things that you do.
A friend is someone who knows how you
Feel when you don't tell him.

A friend is someone you tell things to
That you don't want others to know.
A friend is someone who will
Accept you in spite of your behavior.
Chorus
A friend is someone who will understand
Your touch on his shoulder the warmth of your hand.
A friend is someone you like to be with.

A friend is someone you give yourself to
Without demanding that they give back to you.
A friend is someone you share with . . .
I share this song with you.

60

WIND AND CLOUDS

In this unit you will find creative ways to teach your students about the weather along with various ideas that can be applied to the theme of wind and clouds.

WIND AND CLOUD RACE

You will need styrofoam cups, some string, a pencil, and tape. Make a hole in the center of the bottom of each cup with the pencil. Cut two pieces of string about two feet in length. Set a large box on a table. Put a string through each cup, taping the strings to the box and the table.

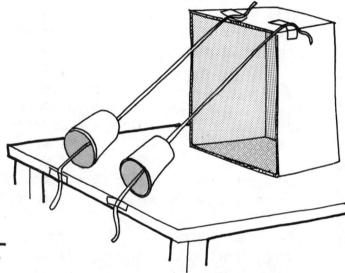

Have the children pretend that they are the wind and blow the cups (clouds). Have them pair up and see whose cloud is first to the top!

CLOUD WATCHING

Take the class cloud watching! Imagine that the clouds are creatures, people, or painted scenes. Have them lie on their backs and watch the clouds move and change shapes. Ask them questions like, "Do clouds travel because the wind blows them?" If it is a rainy day, watch the clouds from your classroom window.

Make bubble paint (see page 13) and paint some cloud scenes.

WIND AND CLOUDS GAME

Have the children stand in a group facing you. When you call "clouds," have them walk very slowly in place. When you call "wind," have them run in place with quick steps. When you call "lightning," have them twist their bodies in different directions. When you call "rain," have them fall to the floor and lie very still.

MAKE A WINDY DAY FUN WITH PINWHEELS

Cut a six-inch or eight-inch square from colored paper. Trace around a penny in the center of the square.

Decorate the front and back of the square with designs or stick stars on the square.

Make diagonal cuts from each corner to the edge of the penny circle. Bend each alternate corner into the center and stick a pin through all four corners into the center. Put the pin into the eraser end of a pencil.

Blow on your pinwheel and watch it spin! Or take it outdoors on a windy day. See what happens to the design. Does the color or shape change?

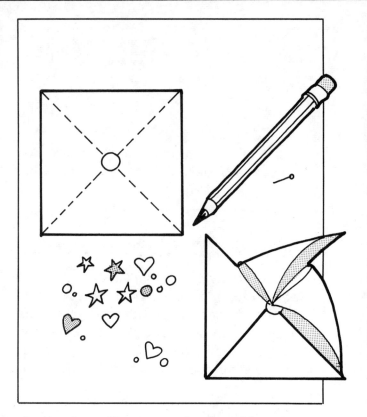

Discuss with your class about kites, windmills, pinwheels, sailboats, and other things that need wind power to make them operate. Have them bring in pictures.

Explain and demonstrate evaporation by washing a spot on the chalkboard and blowing it dry.

Trivia Question: Why is it that sometimes when it rains there aren't any clouds?

Answer: Because the clouds are several miles above the ground and it is a long way for the rain to fall. Sometimes the cloud disappears by the time the rain reaches the ground.

Read to the class *The Wind Thief* by Judi Barrett, Atheneum, New York, 1977.

Did you know that drops of water in clouds are so tiny that more than 100 million of them could be put in a teaspoon?

PARACHUTE FUN ON A WINDY DAY

Have each child make a parachute that will float down from the sky with its passenger. Tie four strong pieces of string, each about nine inches long, to the corners of a handkerchief. Fasten a tin soldier or small lightweight toy character to the opposite ends of the strings. Roll it carefully in the parachute. When it is thrown into the air, it will drift to Earth.

Discuss how heavy things fall faster than lightweight items. What makes the parachute float?

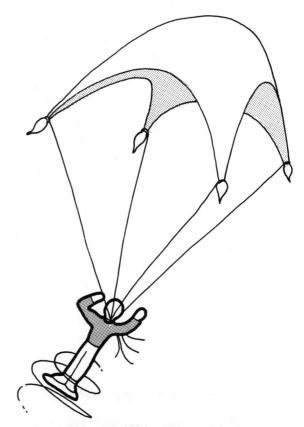

WINDMILL GAME

Have the children choose partners and stand back-to-back, stretching their arms out at their sides. Have them bend down and touch the right leg with the right hand and then the left leg with the left hand. Moving together, each pair makes a windmill.

MAKING A WINDMILL

Fill a one-quart milk carton with sand or rocks.

Cut slits in a paper plate. Twist the cut places all going in the same direction.

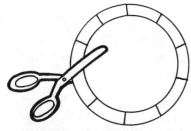
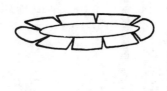

Attach the paper plate to the milk carton by sticking a large pin through the plate and then through a bead and into the carton.

Make your windmill go around!

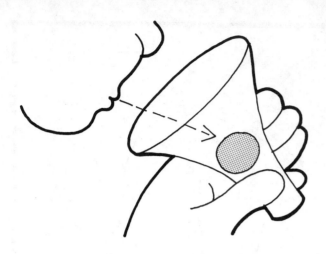

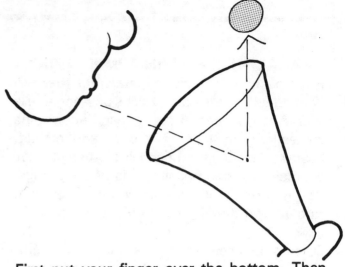

WHO CAN BLOW THE BALL OUT?

Roll a small piece of aluminum foil into a ball. Drop it in a funnel. See who can blow it out.

No one can blow it out! Explain that the wind goes around the ball and out the bottom of the funnel.

First put your finger over the bottom. Then blow. Now the ball can be blown out!

CLOUD PICTURES

Look at and study the shapes of clouds. Have your class draw pictures of clouds with chalk, paint, crayon, or felt-tip pens. They can glue their cloud pictures inside a decorated box lid and hang them up around the room.

FINGER-PAINT CLOUDS

Have the children finger-paint some clouds on the classroom windows with spray-on shaving cream. When they're done finger-painting, the shaving cream will wash right off!

Trivia Question: Can you walk through a cloud?

Answer: You are walking through a cloud when you walk through fog, and you feel the dampness of tiny droplets on your hands and face.

On a very cold day, you form a little cloud every time your moist breath hits the cold air.

Clouds are made of millions of tiny drops of water which float in the air.

FALLING CLOUDS GAME

Choose two children to form a cloud. As they hold their arms up high with hands locked, the rest of the class marches in a circle to music under the cloud. When the music stops, the children who form the cloud will put their arms down. The child caught in the cloud goes to the center of the circle. When a second child is caught by the cloud, he and the child in the center of the circle form a new cloud. The game continues until five clouds have been formed.

"The wind is like a circus clown"
(arms extended, waving as desired)
"Who tumbles things all upside down."
(somersault or place head down and touch hands to floor)
"He grabs my hat and runs away
In his jolly autumn play."
(grab hat to keep it from blowing off head, then run in small circle)
"He makes the leaves around me jig,"
(jump in place in following manner:
right foot forward on *makes*
left foot forward on *leaves*
right foot forward on *around*
left foot forward on *jig*)
"and twists me like a whirligig."
(whirl around on one toe and stop on *whirligig*)
"I love the clown of autumn days
Though he teases many ways."
(Again extend arms, swinging them around as desired and make funny clown faces. Stop on the word *ways* like a soldier at attention with no smile—nothing)

CLOWNISH WIND

Words by Helen Kitchell Evans
Music by Frances Mann Benson

The wind (sing or whistle like) is like a cir-cus clown who tum-bles things all up-side down. He grabs my hat and runs a-way in his jol-ly aut-umn play. He makes the leaves around me jig. And twists me like a whirl-i-gig. I love the clown of aut-umn days. Tho he teas-es man-y ways.

CREATIVE WRITING: ADVENTURES IN THE WIND
PAPER WIND SOCK

Have each student select one of the following to write a story about and illustrate it. These are just some thoughts to include in the stories. Encourage students to be creative in telling their adventures.

Pretend you are a leaf blowing in the wind. What kinds of adventures do you have? Where does the wind take you? Whom do you see? Are you afraid or are you excited about the adventure?

Pretend you are hanging onto the tail of a kite. Where would you fly to? What would you see? How would you feel blowing around in the sky? What adventures would you have? What lands would you fly over?

Pretend you are a kite blowing in the wind. What kind of a kite are you? To whom do you belong? Will you win the kite contest? How high and wild does the wind blow you?

Trivia Question: Which comes first—the lightning or the thunder?
Answer: As tiny drops of water in a cloud move through the air, they become charged with electricity. When the charge in a cloud becomes great enough, a spark jumps from the cloud. As the spark goes through the air, it warms it. The air expands and rushes outward causing the sound waves we hear called "thunder." Thunder always comes after the lightning has flashed. So don't be afraid of thunder. Thunder is not dangerous.

LET THE CHILDREN MAKE THEIR OWN LIGHTNING!

You will need two small balloons shaped like sausages. Blow them up and tie knots in the ends. This experiment must be done in a room which is completely dark.

Have each child rub the balloons back and forth against his clothing. Rub both balloons at the same time. Then bring them together so that they almost touch. Children will see small flashes of light as the electricity jumps between the balloons, and they will hear a faint crackle. They can take turns and do this over and over again.

CRUNCHY BREAD STICKS FOR A WINDY DAY

4 slices of bread
Soft margarine
Garlic salt or Parmesan cheese

Heat oven to 350°. Spread soft margarine over each slice of bread. Set the bread on a cutting board and cut into long thin strips. Sprinkle each strip with garlic salt or Parmesan cheese before baking (if desired). Place strips on cookie sheet and bake for twenty minutes or until brown. Makes approximately thirty-two crunchy bread sticks. Delightful warm treat for a windy day!

CLOUDBURSTS CHOCOLATE PEANUT BUTTER CLOUDS

1 lb. powdered sugar
1 cup melted chocolate
1 ¼ cups graham cracker crumbs
1 ½ cups peanut butter
12-oz. pkg. chocolate chips
1 jar marshmallow topping

Combine first four ingredients and press into a 9" x 13" pan. Melt a package of chocolate chips and spread over the mixture. Drop marshmallow topping by teaspoonful over the chocolate, making small white clouds. Refrigerate. Cut into squares or cut into cloud shapes and refrigerate again.

TIN CANS WIND CHIME

Save many different shapes and sizes of tin cans. Wash them clean and remove labels.

Decorate tin cans with (1) waterproof felt-tip markers, (2) spray paint, or (3) glued-on colored paper with pretty designs (can't hang these outside on a rainy day).

Punch two holes at the top of each can and attach string or yarn to hang them up. Hang in a group from a stick close enough to touch when they move in the breeze. Can hang in a window or doorway, on a patio or porch, or from a tree branch.

Bulletin Board Idea

Preparation:
Cover the bulletin board with light-blue paper. Have the class make creative and colorful kites. Attach kites to the bulletin board. Use ribbon for the tails. By using a fan or some other device, create a breeze to blow the kites. Attach appropriate lettering. Display good work papers on the colorful kites.

SOAR ABOVE THE CLOUDS WITH GOOD STUDY HABITS

Be neat

Concentrate on the lesson

Find time to study

Sit correctly

Have a good attitude

Hold pencil correctly

Form letters properly

Preparation:
Cover the bulletin board with light-blue paper. Attach white fluffy clouds made from construction paper to the blue paper. Inside each cloud write a good study habit. Attach appropriate lettering.

PAPER WIND SOCK

Cut five strips of lightweight paper, each a different color, 12" x 4".
Glue each strip together.
Glue five strips to each other.

Cut eight colored strips, 12" x 2".
Glue these eight strips on bottom ring of wind sock.

Attach string in top ring for hanging.

Hang wind socks up in the classroom.

Write poems about windy days on the colored strips of paper before gluing together.

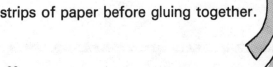

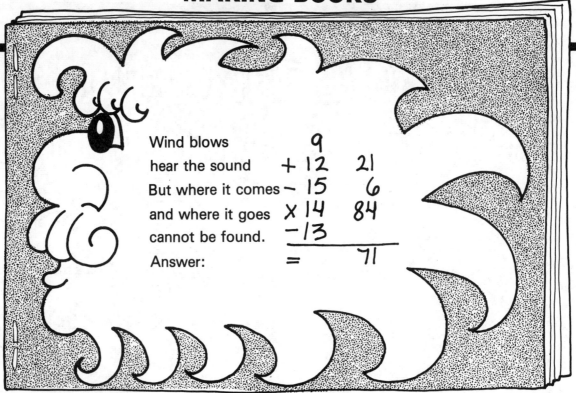

Wind blows		9
hear the sound	+ 12	21
But where it comes	− 15	6
and where it goes	× 14	84
cannot be found.	− 13	
Answer:	=	71

Have the class draw pictures of "old man wind" on the cover for a book and work out a game. This is a book for spelling-arithmetic games about the wind. The teacher will read the poem, a line at a time. The students will write it as the teacher reads it, writing one line under the other. Tell them to spell the words carefully as this is important to their answers. When they have finished writing, tell them to count the number of letters in each line and write the number after each line. When everyone is ready, you will tell them what to do with each number. Explain that sometimes they will add, or subtract, or sometimes multiply, or divide the numbers. That is why it is important to spell the words correctly. Explain that if they misspell a word, they may not have the right number of letters, so they cannot work out the problem correctly. There is a chance, however, that they might misspell a word but still have the right number of letters in it. In that case they could get the correct answer to the arithmetic problem. So, they will score a point for a correct answer and an extra point for spelling all the words correctly. Put a similar example for them on the board first.

Have the children write short simple poems about windy days and make up their own problems for inside the book. Answers could be put on the reverse side of each problem. Put the books in your library for the class to share.

Board Example:

Gentle Wind		10
where do you hide?	+ 14	24
I feel your touch	− 14	10
at my side.	× 8	
Answer:	= 80	

EXPERIMENT: MAKING CLOUDS

Discuss with the class that clouds are composed of water and how temperature affects cloud formation.

For this experiment you will need a glass container with a wide mouth, hot water, ice cubes, a lamp, and a flat glass cover for the glass container.

The students will observe the formation of a cloud in the glass container as you pour about two inches of hot water into the glass container. Put the lid on and let it sit for three to nine minutes. Now place ice cubes on the lid. Darken the room and hold a lamp behind the bottle. A cloud will be forming. Discuss that as the moisture that has been vaporized cools due to the ice cubes, it forms clouds of moisture. This is how real clouds form.

WIND STRENGTH

Discuss with your class that air is real and can move objects. A strong wind (especially hurricanes or tornadoes) can blow objects over or move them.

Set two heavy books close together standing on their ends, on a table. Let the children try to blow either one over. Now tell the class you are going to blow it over. Blow up a balloon between the two books. Your breath fills the balloon and a book falls over.

MAKE YOUR OWN WIND VANE

You can make a simple instrument to help you determine from which direction the wind blows.

You will need a drinking straw, a feather, a cardboard paper arrowhead, a straight pin, pencil with an eraser, and a long stick.

In one end of the straw, put a feather; and in the other end, put a paper arrowhead. Stick the pin through the middle of the straw and into the eraser. Attach the pencil to a long stick. Make the letters N, S, E, W for North, South, East, and West from paper. Tape them on the pencil being careful that they face in the right direction.

Have your students take their wind vanes outside on a windy day. The straw will turn when the wind blows and point in its direction. Discuss the relationships between the difference of the wind and the weather and temperature.

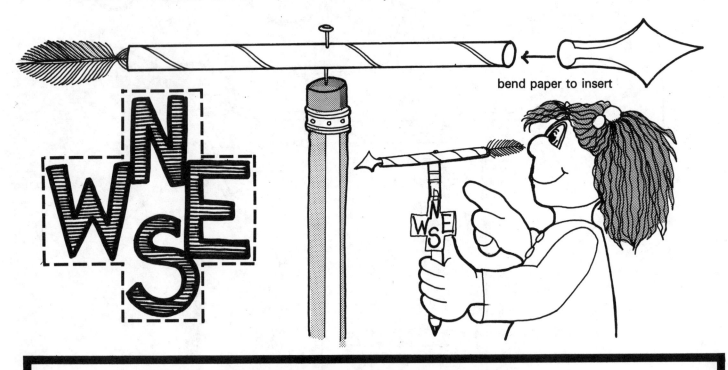

bend paper to insert

WEATHER WORD SEARCH

Have your students make up their own word searches by using words that have to do with weather. Copy them off and let them exchange and work each other's.

Some weather words might be:

cloudy	frost	sun
rain	sleet	ice
snow	dew	humidity
moisture	breeze	fog
windy	hurricane	lightning
hail	thunder	cold

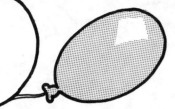

BALLOONS

Balloons always create an atmosphere of excitement. Your students will enjoy learning as you use balloons for a teaching tool in your classroom.

ILLUSTRATE OR DRAMATIZE

Have the children draw pictures to illustrate this poem, or have them act it out.

The Balloon Man

See the balloon man with his balloons;
He holds them on a string.
He whistles happy tunes and walks about,
Through puddles in the spring.

In the wind the balloons do bob
And tug above his head;
Green balloons and blue balloons,
And yellow ones, and red.

He takes our quarters and unties,
The two we choose, and then
He tips his hat and waves his hand
And whistles once again.

Karan Gleason

RAINY DAY BALLOON CREATURES

Here's a fun way to celebrate a special day or the last day of school.

Put some confetti in the balloons before you blow them up. Inflate the balloons and tie the ends in knots.

Decorate the balloons with felt-tip pens, glitter, stickers, etc., creating balloon creatures.

Tie a ribbon, yarn, or curling ribbon on the end of each balloon and hang from the ceiling lights. When you break the balloons, it will rain confetti to celebrate the occasion!

STORY STARTERS

Balloons can be used for many learning activities. Write enough story starters for the entire class on small pieces of paper. Fold them and place one in each balloon. Blow up the balloons and tie the ends in knots. Have each student select a balloon as he goes to recess. Outside he will break his balloon and save the story starter to write the story in class.

LOST BALLOONS

Fill large sturdy balloons with helium. Have each child write a message on a postcard and address the postcard to himself. The message should ask that the finder of the balloon mail the card back to the child, telling where it was found and something about himself. Laminate all the postcards to protect them from the weather, and tie them to the balloons. Take the balloons outside and release them all together. What a fun way to make new friends! And it'll be exciting to see whose balloon travelled the farthest!

BALLOON RELAYS

Choose two teams and have each form a line. Give the first player in each line a balloon. On signal, have the first player bat the balloon with his hand while running to the other end of the room and back to the next player, who repeats the action. Continue until all the children have had a turn. The team finishing first wins.

Variations: (1) Each player kicks the balloon to the end of the room and back. (Balloon may be touched only with feet and legs.) (2) With a balloon between each player's knees, he must hop to the end of the room and back; and after crossing the finish line, hand the balloon to the next player. If a balloon is dropped, it must be put back in place before hopping.

74

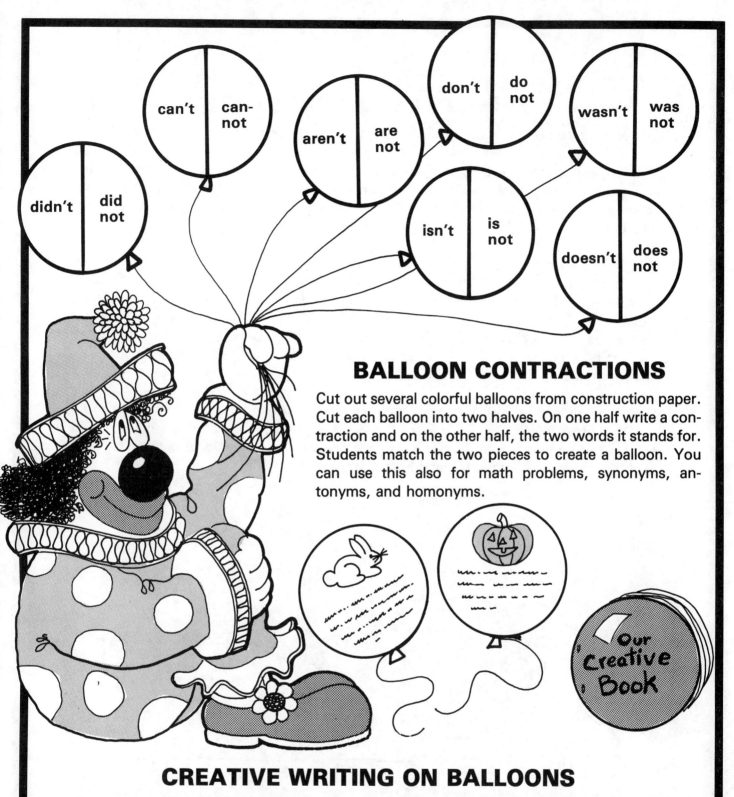

BALLOON CONTRACTIONS

Cut out several colorful balloons from construction paper. Cut each balloon into two halves. On one half write a contraction and on the other half, the two words it stands for. Students match the two pieces to create a balloon. You can use this also for math problems, synonyms, antonyms, and homonyms.

CREATIVE WRITING ON BALLOONS

Cut out and collect interesting pictures from magazines. Glue each picture at the top of a large construction paper balloon. Have the children create stories about the pictures and write them on the balloons. Keep all class stories and make a creative writing book for your classroom library, or put the stories up on the bulletin board.

BALLOON CATCH GAME

Have the children sit in a circle. Give each a number. Throw a balloon into the air, and at the same time call out a number. The student whose number is called must catch the balloon before it touches the floor.

EFFECTS OF AIR PRESSURE

Is it possible to see snow on a mountain with flowers growing in a valley below?

High up, where the air is thinner, there are fewer molecules to bump against each other and heat up. Nearer to the earth, where the molecules are squeezed close together, they collide more often and become hotter. Try this experiment with your class to show what happens.

First fill a balloon with dried navy beans. Then blow it up and hold it at the neck so that the air cannot escape. Shake the balloon lightly. The beans will bounce about like air molecules which are always on the move. As they bounce back and forth, they will bump into one another and the children will hear a clicking sound. The more beans you are able to squeeze into the balloon before it is blown up, the more clicks there will be. Now you can see how molecules of air, squeezed together close to the earth, rub against each other more often and how they become hotter.

So it is possible to see two different effects of air pressure in the same part of the country. You can see snow on a mountaintop, where the air is thin and molecules are far apart, while flowers are growing in a warm valley beneath, where molecules of air have been squeezed tightly together and heated up.

BACK-TO-BACK BALLOON RACE

Choose two teams and have students pair up with partners. Have the pairs stand in a line, back-to-back, with a balloon held between their backs. On signal, the first pair should press together and race to the other end of the room and back. If the balloon falls or breaks, they have to start over. The winner is the team that finishes first.

HAVE YOU SEEN MY BALLOON?

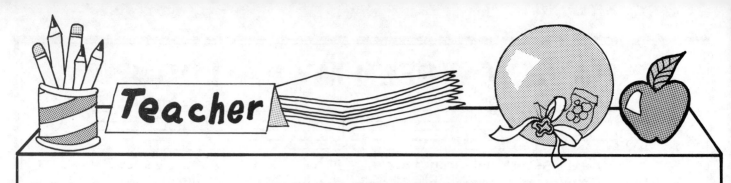

BALLOON TREAT

Here's a special treat for teacher or students to give, or to use for Open House as name cards on desks.

Fold a small fun-size package of M & M's candy and stuff inside a balloon. Blow up the balloon and tie the end in a knot. The weight of the candy will hold the balloon on a desk.

Write a message on the balloon, or draw pictures with black felt-tip pen. When balloon is popped, a treat is left!

BALLOON BLOWING

Divide the class into two teams and place them on opposite ends of a wide table. Put a balloon in the center. On signal, they try to blow the balloon over the heads of their opponents. When this is done, that team receives a point. Game is ten points.

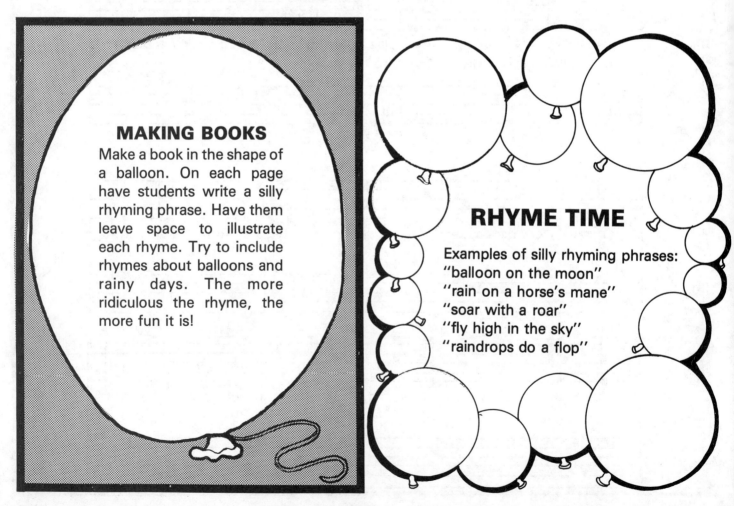

MAKING BOOKS

Make a book in the shape of a balloon. On each page have students write a silly rhyming phrase. Have them leave space to illustrate each rhyme. Try to include rhymes about balloons and rainy days. The more ridiculous the rhyme, the more fun it is!

RHYME TIME

Examples of silly rhyming phrases:
"balloon on the moon"
"rain on a horse's mane"
"soar with a roar"
"fly high in the sky"
"raindrops do a flop"

PICK A BALLOON FOR CREATIVE WRITING

Pick a balloon and write a creative story from one of the ideas.

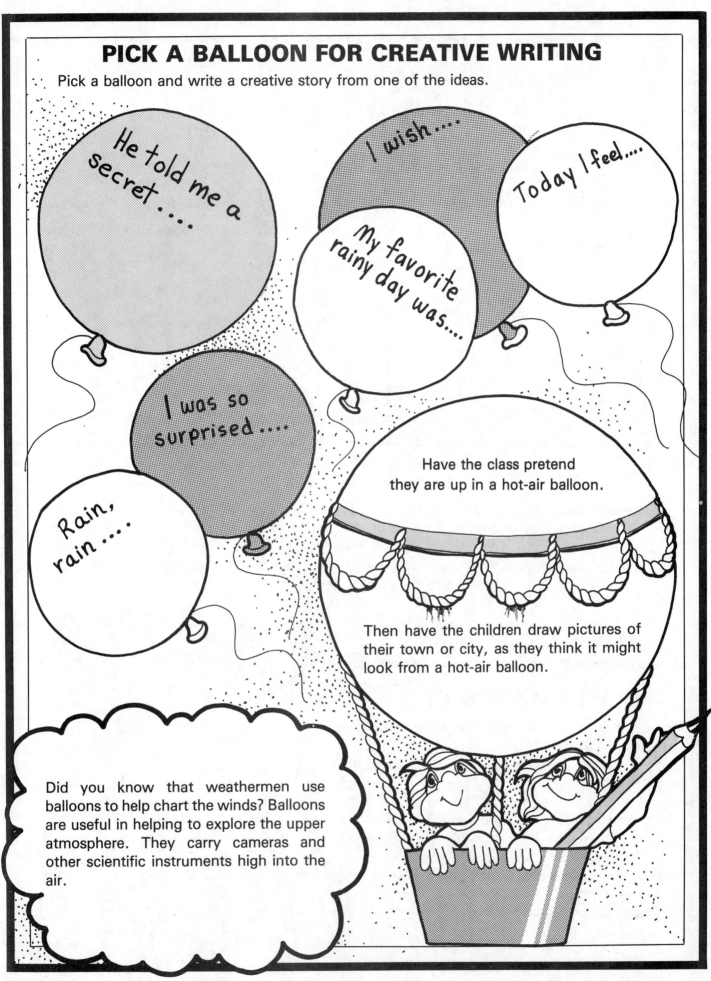

He told me a secret....

I wish....

Today I feel....

My favorite rainy day was....

I was so surprised....

Rain, rain....

Have the class pretend they are up in a hot-air balloon.

Then have the children draw pictures of their town or city, as they think it might look from a hot-air balloon.

Did you know that weathermen use balloons to help chart the winds? Balloons are useful in helping to explore the upper atmosphere. They carry cameras and other scientific instruments high into the air.

Preparation:
Draw a silhouette of city buildings along the bottom border of a bulletin board. Cut out various colorful balloons with classroom goals written on them and attach them to the bulletin board. Attach appropriate lettering. You can coordinate bulletin board with weekly goals set by students in the activity below.

WEEKLY GOALS

Have the children write their names on inflated balloons with felt-tip markers. Attach each balloon to a dowel rod or a stick and tape to each student's desk.

Then have the children select goals they would like to accomplish for the week. Discuss the bulletin board goals above. At the end of the week, if a goal has been met, the student can pop his balloon which indicates success in meeting that goal.

BALLOON CROSSWORD PUZZLE

Across:
2. To explode
4. Drifting gently in the air
5. Air in motion
7. A gas used for inflating balloons
8. The act of flying

Down:
1. To fly high into the air
2. An inflatable rubber bag
3. To blow full with air or gas
6. A thin line of fiber used for tying

CRUNCHY CHEESE KRISPIES

1 stick soft margarine
10 oz. Cracker Barrel cheddar cheese, grated
1 cup flour
½ tsp. baking powder
¼ tsp. salt
1 tsp. grated onion (if desired)
1 cup Rice Krispies

Cream margarine and cheese. Stir in dry ingredients and onion. Add Rice Krispies. Roll into balls the size of large marbles. Press flat with thumb on an ungreased baking sheet. Bake at 325° for 10—12 minutes. Makes about five dozen. Can be frozen. Cheese krispies puff up like orange balloons! Nutritious, delicious, and crunchy to eat!

SECRET CODE NUMBERS

Put each problem on a colorful paper balloon with the answer on the back of the balloon. Put the code up in the front of the classroom on a large balloon or on the chalkboard.

Use the code to find the sums.
Skill: Sums to 17
(Can do the same for subtraction.)

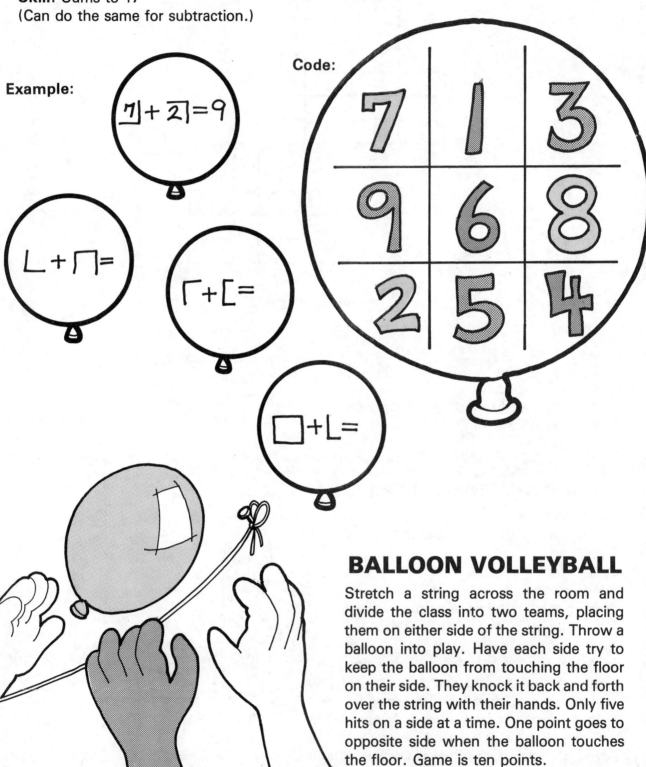

Example:

Code:

$⌐\hspace{-0.1em}| + ⌐\hspace{-0.1em}2 = 9$

L + ⊓ =

Γ + ⊏ =

☐ + L =

7	1	3
9	6	8
2	5	4

BALLOON VOLLEYBALL

Stretch a string across the room and divide the class into two teams, placing them on either side of the string. Throw a balloon into play. Have each side try to keep the balloon from touching the floor on their side. They knock it back and forth over the string with their hands. Only five hits on a side at a time. One point goes to opposite side when the balloon touches the floor. Game is ten points.

"B" BALLOONS

Have the children cut out balloon shapes from colored construction paper and attach yarn to them.

Ask them to write words that start with "B" on their paper balloon and to illustrate their words.

Use these "B" words and drawings to make a bulletin board or hang from your ceiling lights.

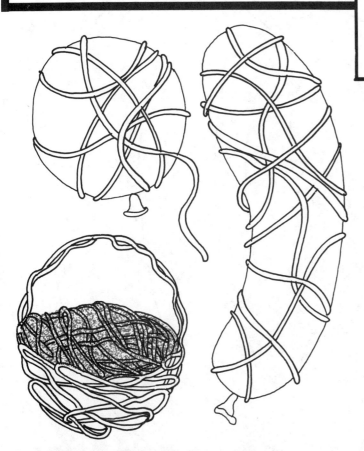

BALLOON SCULPTURES

Blow up various sizes and shapes of balloons. Dip yarn or string in plaster of Paris and wrap around a balloon. After the yarn or string dries, pop the balloon and a sculpture has been created.

A fun way to make Easter baskets in the shape of an egg.

BALLOON MATH

With a felt-tip pen, write one numeral on each paper balloon or on real balloons. Students can find the total of all the balloons and make as many math sentences as possible using the numerals on the balloons. Ask questions such as, what is the total of all blue balloons? How much more is the total of the green balloons than the total of the orange ones?

BALLOON MAZE

Start at the arrow and find your way through the balloon to the end.

START

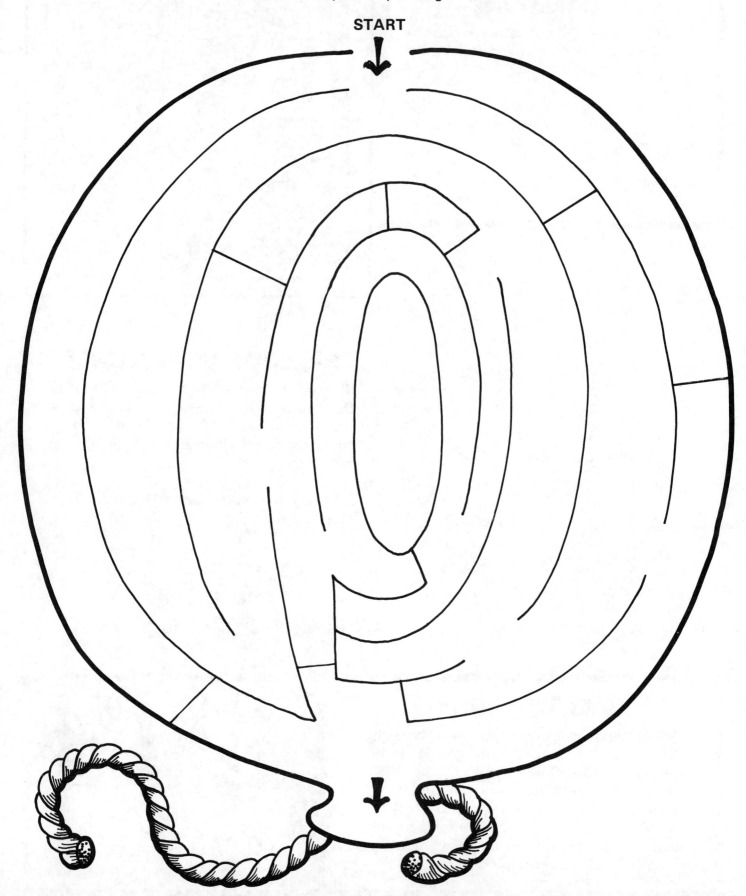

TURTLES, DUCKS, AND FROGS

These rainy day creatures generate enthusiasm into learning experiences, especially for the early learners. Math and English teaching techniques are integrated with bulletin boards, awards, games, craft ideas, recipes, science projects, and puppets to create an atmosphere that learning is fun.

FOOD BINGO

Make Bingo cards in the shape of turtles, using reading words. The youngest children would do best with only nine words. Use finger food like dry cereal, nuts, or small marshmallows as markers. When the session is over, the children may eat them.

Variation: Bingo cards may contain spelling words or words from a poem the class is studying. The teacher reads lines or phrases of the poem, and students cover any words from that line or phrase that are on their cards.

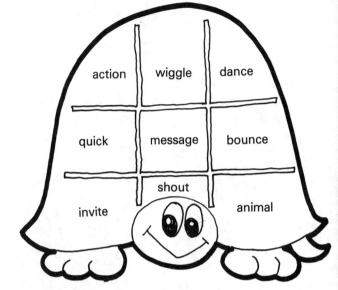

TURTLE, DUCK, AND FROG RHYMES

Have the students finish the following rhymes any way they like:

Possible rhyming words are:

1. It's raining, it's raining the little duck cried,

   _____.

   hide   fried
   ride   sighed

2. Quacking ducks splashing in puddles,

   _____.

   cuddles   huddles
   muddles

3. A big green frog sat croaking on a lily pad,

   _____.

   fad   mad
   bad   lad

4. A pet frog would be such fun,

   _____.

   won   sun
   ton   run

5. Jolly little raindrops fell on turtle's back,

   _____.

   tack   sack
   pack   lack

6. Hurry little turtle, come be my friend,

   _____.

   send   lend
   tend   bend

Draw and cut out large turtles, ducks, and frogs, and have the children write their finished rhymes on the appropriate animals. Hang these rhymes from the ceiling lights with yarn.

LISTEN AND LIST

Read the class a poem on turtles, ducks, or frogs.

Have the students listen and write down action words, nouns, adjectives, etc. Make a list on the board from their lists.

Suggested Poem:
"The Duck" by Edith King
The Home Book of Verse for Young Folks by Burton E. Stevenson, Henry Holt & Co., 1945.

HOP-CLAP FROGS

Form a circle with the players standing about three feet apart. On signal have them place their hands on their hips and stoop down until they are almost sitting on their heels. Tell them to start hopping around the circle in one direction, clapping their hands first in front of them and then behind them. The players must continue to stoop while they hop. Anyone who tips over must leave the circle. The last one to continue hopping without falling over is the winner. Great for coordination!

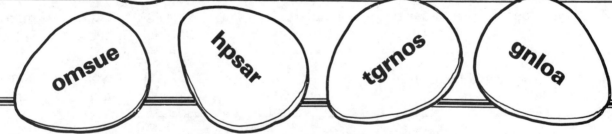

SCRAMBLED DUCK EGGS

Using the spelling words for the week, mix up or scramble the letters in each word. Write these words on egg shapes and distribute to your students. Have them figure out the correct spelling on a sheet of paper. After a few seconds exchange eggs and try a new word. After awhile give the correct spellings to see how many they guessed correctly.

Suggested Reading:
The Little Duck Who Loved Rain by Peter Mabie, Wilcox & Follet Co., Chicago.

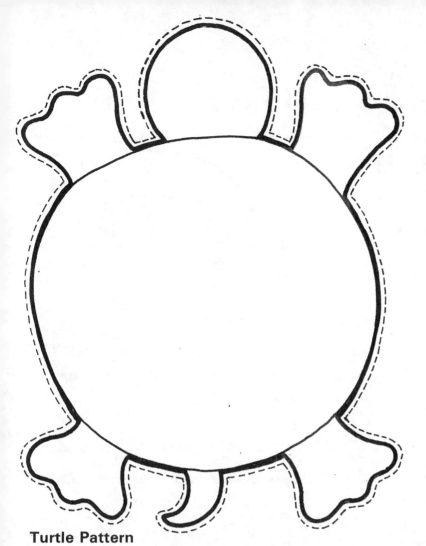

Turtle Pattern

MAKING BOOKS

Adopt a class turtle. Check books out of the library on turtles and learn about them.

Make this book in the shape of a turtle. Have the children record all they learn about turtles in their books.

Have them write poems about turtles on the front covers of their books.

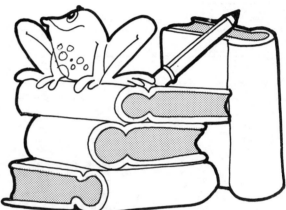

RAINY DAY ANIMAL POP-UP PUPPETS

Poke a hole through an egg carton cup and push a straw through it, taping it securely inside. Now poke a hole in the bottom of the paper cup and put the other end of the straw through it.

Use construction paper and crayons to make cutouts of turtles, ducks, and frogs. Glue these onto the egg cup.

Push the straw up and down and your puppet will pop up and talk to you.

Have the students create rainy day stories about turtles, ducks, and frogs. These puppets are perfect to use in a car while traveling!

← **egg cup**

← **paper cup**

AWARDS

(to go with bulletin board themes on following page)

Quacking Up over the Best Reader Congratulations! to

_____

_____ Books Read

_____ Date

_____ Teacher

Something to Hop About! Congratulations! to

_____

For: _____

Date: _____

From: _____

(Also, give as an award to the winner of "Hop-Clap Frogs" game on page 86.)

Good Manners Award to

_____

Date: _____

From: _____

Congratulations!

Preparation:
Draw a large duck and attach to board along with appropriate lettering. Mount pictures the students have drawn which illustrate books they have read.

More Bulletin Board Ideas

1. Frog Bulletin Board: Attach a large frog and letters to a bulletin board that reads . . . "Something to Hop About!" You can mount frog poems or stories, good papers, or drawings.

2. Turtle-Duck-Frog Bulletin Board: Attach lettering that reads . . . "Watch Your Manners." Put on the board turtles, ducks, and frogs playing in and around a large pond. On lily pads write expressions such as May I? Thank you! Please! Excuse me! which show good manners and scatter lily pads on the pond.

ANIMAL MATH STORIES

A simple story started by the teacher and continued by the students can become a fun learning event as it is illustrated on a flannel board.

Make a flannel board out of a heavy piece of cardboard by covering it with flannel. Glue the flannel in place. Cut turtles, ducks, and frogs out of felt for your stories.

Start the story and place the correct animal or animals on the board. Call on the children to come up and continue the story while they place their animals on the board.

Variations: Cut numbers out of felt. Have the children match numbers to the numbers of animals on the board or vice versa. May add and subtract animals.

TRANSPARENT-CREATURES

Cut shapes of turtles, ducks, and frogs from black construction paper, cutting each one double so you end up with two exactly the same. Next cut large holes in each shape in the spots you want to see through.

Now cut pieces of colored cellophane large enough to cover each hole. On one of the shapes, brush rubber cement around the outside edge of each hole and lay the cellophane pieces over the holes. Press firmly until they stick.

After each hole is covered with cellophane, brush rubber cement around the edge of the shape. The cement should be put on the same side you pasted the colored cellophane. Lay the second shape on top of the one with the wet cement, and press them together.

Hang your transparent creatures up in the classroom windows for all to enjoy!

TURTLE PAPERWEIGHT

Make a paper pattern of this turtle in the size and shape shown. Trace around the turtle pattern on a piece of felt or colored paper and cut it out.

Glue empty half-walnut shell, upside down, on the back of the turtle for his shell. Glue sequins on for eyes.

Optional: To use for a paperweight, fill shell with casting plaster first. Mix one tablespoon water for each three tablespoons plaster. Fill walnut shell and set it in the sun to dry. When dry, glue it to the back of the turtle.

DUCK HOMONYMS

Draw and cut out several duck shapes. Write matching homonyms on both sides of the duck.

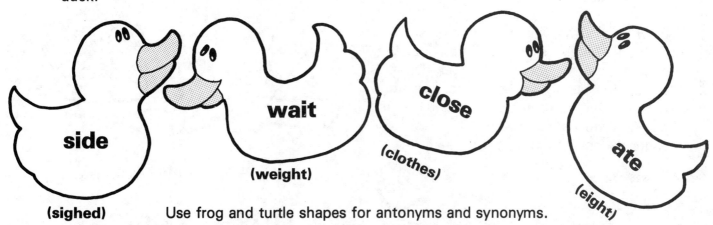

side

(sighed)

wait

(weight)

close

(clothes)

ate

(eight)

Use frog and turtle shapes for antonyms and synonyms.

DUCKS ARE WATERPROOF

Suggested Reading:
Ducks Don't Get Wet by Augusta Goldin
   Thomas Y. Crowell Co., New York, 1965.

Ducks spend most of their time in water, splashing, diving, and paddling about, and yet they never get wet. This book explains why this is so. With a simple experiment explained in the book, the class can prove this. (An excellent read-and-find-out science book about ducks.)

BUTTON-BACKED TURTLES

Have the class bring in some old buttons their mothers do not need. Have the children draw pictures of turtles on construction paper using the buttons to fill in the turtle's shell. You can also use the buttons for eyes and nose.

Discuss large and small sizes of buttons. For younger children, use as a math lesson and count the buttons. Sort according to colors and do math problems.

FROG AND FLIES

The flies form a circle around the frog, who squats in the center. The circle is in the center of the play area, with one border of the play area as a base.

The frog tells the flies how they must move around the circle (skip, hop, etc.) and they continue until he jumps to his feet. The flies then try to get to base before being caught. Those that the frog catches squat and become frogs to help catch the rest. The last child caught becomes the new frog.

TURTLE COOKIES

Here's a fun way to bake cookies.

Melt the unsweetened chocolate with the margarine.

Combine and mix eggs, sugar, salt, flour, and nuts. Add the melted mixture and stir.

Drop the dough by teaspoonfuls on a hot waffle iron and bake for one minute.

Makes sixty "turtle" cookies.

Ingredients:
4 squares unsweetened chocolate
1 cup margarine
4 eggs
1½ cups sugar
½ tsp. salt
2 cups flour
1 cup chopped nuts

MY LITTLE DUCK

Stand the players in a large circle, facing inward and holding hands. Choose one child to walk around outside the circle and repeat over and over, "I am a little duck, but I won't chase you, I won't chase you . . ." Suddenly, he should change the ending by saying, "but I will chase you." Then he quickly lays a scarf on the shoulder of the player he decides to tag. The one tagged must chase him in and out under the arms of the players in the circle and try to tag him before he gets back to the empty place. If tagged, he is the little duck again. If the one tagged doesn't catch the duck, then he is the duck.

TURTLE, TURTLE HIDING BEHIND THE ROCK

This is a terrific game for a rainy day when students bring umbrellas to school.

Send one child out of the room. Pick another child to be the turtle who will hide behind the open umbrella which is a rock. Then have the rest of the class change seats to confuse the guesser.

Now have the person outside come in and try to guess within ten seconds who is hiding behind the umbrella.

RAINY DAY WITH MOBILE

Learning to count can be fun this colorful way.

Cut out various numbers of ducks, frogs, turtles, and raindrops. String them on sewing thread and tie them to the bottom of a coat hanger.

Cover the open area of the coat hanger with paper (sky), cut a little larger all around than the hanger. Apply glue to hanger and lay the paper over it. Repeat on the back side of hanger; then glue cotton clouds on the sky. Hang mobiles up in the classroom.

CAPITALS, NUMBERS, AND CONTRACTIONS

Numbers:
Make twenty turtles. Write numerals 1—10 on half of them and the words *one—ten* on the other half. Have the students match number words and numerals.

Capitals:
Make fifty-two ducks. Write capital letters on half and lowercase letters on the other half. Have the students match duck friends by pairing capital and lowercase letters.

Contractions:
Make several frogs and lily pads. Write contractions on the frogs and the two words that make the contraction on the lily pads. Have the students match each lily pad to its frog contraction.

Suggested Reading:
Did you know that toads protect themselves from other animals with a liquid on their skin that stings the mouth of a predator? Read interesting books about toads such as:

Toad by Anne & Harlow Rockwell, Doubleday & Co., Inc., New York, 1972.

Good reading on turtles:
Let's Get Turtles by Millicent E. Selsam, Harper & Row, New York, 1965.

CLASSROOM HELPERS BOARD

Make a colorful classroom helpers board that can be used all year. Design a large pond and glue it to a thin sheet of steel that has been cut the same size. Attach to a bulletin board.

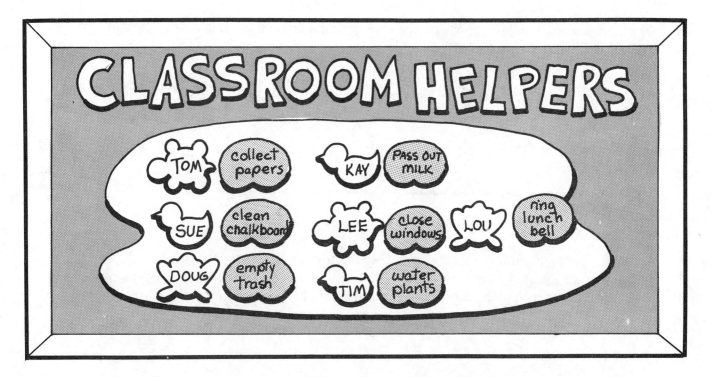

Cut out strips of paper or lily pads and label each, using a black felt-tip pen, with a classroom job. Laminate them and attach a small strip of magnetic tape to the back of each. Distribute the jobs around the pond.

Divide your class evenly into turtles, ducks, and frogs. Cut out that number of colorful turtles, ducks, and frogs and write each child's name on a paper animal with black felt-tip pen. Laminate the animals and attach a small strip of magnetic tape to the back of each. Put turtles, ducks, and frogs near the jobs. You can easily change animals each week to a different job.

ANIMAL IMITATIONS

Ask: How many animal movements can you make? The little children especially love to imitate animal movements and sounds.

1. Can you waddle like a duck?
2. Can you hop like a frog?
3. Can you pull your head inside your house like a turtle?

Add other animals they can imitate.

TURTLES, DUCKS, AND FROGS MOBILES

Have the children cut large double shapes of turtles, ducks, and frogs from tissue paper. Staple one edge and stuff the shape with one more tissue paper. Staple all the edges together and hang the completed animals from the ceiling on a coat hanger.

You can use all three in a mobile or just one kind of animal and make them different sizes. Have the children learn how to balance a mobile.

CREATIVE WRITING

Read the story of the *Turtle and the Hare* to the class. Using that theme, have your students make up their own stories, possibly with a surprise ending, about the slowpoke turtle and the fast hopping frog. These stories could be acted out using two characters.

SLOWPOKE TURTLE

Here's a turtle they can make to go with their story.

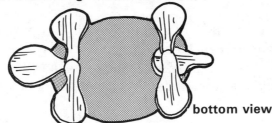
bottom view

Paint a large, smooth stone with green paint. When it is dry, paint a light-green shell design on the top of the stone. Paint shell markings on top of the shell design. Let them be creative in these designs. When the stone is dry, turn it upside down.

Paint six small wooden ice-cream spoons green. Glue one spoon on for the head, with the large end sticking out. Opposite, glue another spoon on for the tail, with the narrow end sticking out (handle part). Make the front legs by gluing the handles of two spoons to the handle of the spoon that forms the head. Make the back legs by gluing the handles of two spoons to the back of the spoon that forms the tail. Let dry overnight.

Add two eyes to the head of the turtle with white paint and make black pupils in the eyes.

RAINY DAY DREAMING

Daydreaming and innovative ways to use the imagination nurture the spirit of creativity. Children love to live in a world of fantasy—a world they can design in the halls of their imaginations. This unit presents ideas for you to use to help stimulate and challenge their imaginations and arouse their worlds of fantasy.

MAKING BOOKS

Make this book in the shape of a dreamy cloud.

On the cloud write a poem about dreaming.

Inside your book write about:
1. What are your dreams for the present?
2. What are your dreams for the future?
3. What are your dreams for making the world a better place for everyone to live?
4. Do you think dreams come true? Explain.

Suggested Reading:
Daydreamers by Eloise Greenfield, Dial Books for Young Readers, New York, 1981.

FANTASY FORT

Create an indoor fort at home or school on a rainy day!

Collect old sheets or blankets for draping. You will need rubber bands or string to fasten sheets to chair backs, table legs, or beds.

Now gather together your favorite toys, treasures, a pillow, and a yummy snack. Have fun in your fantasy fort!

Or close your eyes and whoooshh! You're off into a world of fantasy. You can pretend almost anything. Imagine Alice who fell down the rabbit hole; or the Velveteen Rabbit being loved and held ever so tightly; or riding the Black Stallion on an island.

BEST DREAM

Draw the best dream you ever had and write a story about it.

ADD-TO-IT STORY

This is a learning game.
Divide the class into groups with six children each. On a paper, each child writes the beginning of an adventure story. Every two to three minutes stories are to be passed to the person on the right. Have each add an exciting incident to each story as it is passed. When each child gets his own story back, he is to write the ending and read his own story aloud.

YOUR WISH IS YOUR COMMAND!

Ask your class, "Would you like to ride on a magic carpet? Would you like to pretend you're a bird gliding through the sky?" You can. There's a mime inside each of you, and with mime, anything is possible. All you need is your body and your imagination! Mime is creating fantasy with illusion. As your body shapes the illusion, the fantasy becomes reality. Mime is silent communication. It is a game everyone can play.

Mime is an exciting and fun way for children to work out their fantasies and to explore their imaginations. Check out a book at the library and learn how to do basic techniques and games in mime with your class.

Suggested Reading:
Mime by Kay Hamblin, Doubleday & Co., New York, 1978.

SECRET DREAMS

Here's a fun way to send a secret message! Tell the children they can create a hidden message with a white crayon, watercolors and a brush.

Begin by writing the message about a secret dream with white crayon on a piece of paper. Using the white crayon, draw a pretty border around the message.

Give the sheet to a friend and ask him or her to paint over the entire area with watercolors and poof! Before your very eyes the hidden message will appear. Create secret dreams to share with all your friends!

Suggested Reading:
For a wonderful adventure and joyful surprise ending (all done in a message in code), read to your class *The Secret Birthday Message* by Eric Carle, Thomas Y. Crowell Co., New York, 1972.

ADVENTURE TIME

It is fun to pretend and use the imagination. Have the children pretend they are having great adventures.

1. Write five adventures you would like to have.
2. Write about one of the imaginary adventures listed in number 1. Be creative.

FANTASY GARDEN

Dampen pieces of brick, clay pot, and sponge and place them in a glass container (an old fishbowl or a large glass jar).

Spatter a few drops of food coloring over the "magic rocks."

Slowly pour on four tablespoons ammonia, four tablespoons liquid bluing, and four tablespoons water being careful not to splash. Then sprinkle salt generously over the top.

Watch your fantasy garden grow! It will take about five hours for this magic garden to grow.

GOOD FAIRY

For younger children's nap time, tell the class the best rester will be chosen to be the good fairy. The good fairy will take her magic wand and awaken the children one at a time. They will quietly get up and put away their blankets and go to their seats. No one may get up until the good fairy has tapped him.

PEEK BOX

Read a story of fantasy or daydreaming. Make a "peek box" by creating a scene of the story in a shoe box.

Take the top off the shoe box and cut a hole in one end of the box.

Have the children create a scene inside the box, facing the hole. Draw pictures, use magazine pictures, or any items they can find for scenery. Place the most important objects near the front. Glue scenery near the back or along the back.

Cut a one-inch slit in the box top for light and tape the top to the shoe box.

On the outside of the box, write what the fantasy or daydream inside is about.

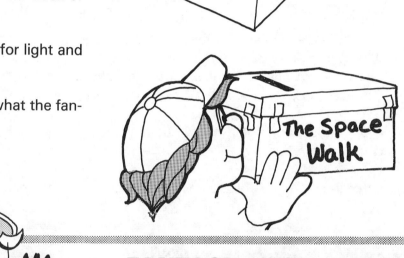

FANTASY BOOK MOBILE

Have the children read different books or poems on fantasy, and then create fantasy book mobiles. They are to show what they read about on the mobiles and hang them up in the classroom.

INVENT A PEACE MACHINE

Imagine that you could invent a spectacular machine that would help the world achieve its dreams of peace and brotherhood. Draw your machine. What would it do? How would it work?

Suggested Reading:
Fun books for children to read to develop their imaginations are those written by Dr. Seuss.

STORYBOOK CHARADES

Children love to hear their favorite stories over and over again. The next time they ask for that special story, ask them to take the parts of the characters. Have a few props handy. The different characters can always be told apart if each one has a hat depicting that character's part in the play. As you read, they will act out the story.

After the students gain confidence in their acting, try having them carry on their play without narration.

Later they may be able to act out stories for each other to guess.

FANTASY SCULPTURES

These creative sculptures come from the students' imaginations and can be whatever they want them to be: animals, unusual designs, or just strange creations. These imaginative sculptures can be enjoyed anytime they feel like a little fantastic daydreaming.

Mix water and plaster of Paris in a coffee can until it looks like cream. Stir continually. Quickly stir enough sand into the mixture until it looks like thick whipped cream. The plaster dries quickly, so work fast.

Pour some of the plaster mixture from the can onto a piece of waxed paper, creating fantasy sculptures or unusual designs. This must be done quickly before the plaster hardens.

When the sculptures have dried, paint and decorate them with poster paints, glitter and sequins. Remove from the waxed paper.

BOOK REPORTS

Have your students read their favorite books. Then they are to make book reports by pretending to be their favorite characters in the books. The children are to dress up like their chosen characters and give oral book reports to the class.

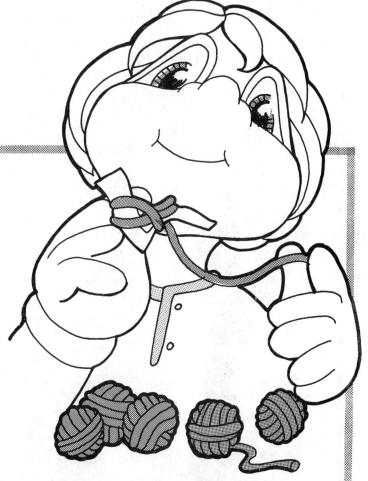

THE WONDER BALL

Write little messages on slips of paper, fold them several times, and one by one, carefully wind yarn around them until each one is completely covered in the ball.

Each child takes a turn unwinding the ball to find a message telling what he must do. It is called the Wonder Ball, because everyone wonders what he will have to do.

Here are a few ways to use the Wonder Ball:
1. Use questions that will reinforce a lesson.
2. Review memory work.
3. Determine classroom job assignments.
4. Tell a story. Hide tiny symbols in the ball and as the children unwind the ball they continue the story or poem, using the symbol they found. It's a fun way to use the imagination and dream up a story together.

BANANA SMOOTHIE

2 peeled bananas
2 cups plain yogurt
1 cup mixed orange juice
2 tbs. honey

Put all the ingredients in a blender and mix until they become a creamy drink. This is a fun recipe to try with different fruits and juices. You can substitute the juice with any of your favorites, as well as try different fruits. Be imaginative and surprise your friends!

FUN SHAPES

See how many interesting things children can dream up from various shapes.

Cut circles, squares, triangles and other shapes from two colors of construction paper, for example, black and white. Cut each shape in half, making one set of shapes from each color.

Children are to use the pieces to assemble their pictures. Tell them to use their imaginations and see what they can create.

PICK A CARD

Dream up lots of things you like to do on a rainy day.

Print one idea on a file card and punch a hole in the center at the top. Either draw pictures on each page to go with the idea or put a pretty border on each card.

Tie all the cards together with yarn. Save the cards for a rainy day when you don't know what to do.

Close your eyes and pick a card. You've found something special to do!

These could be classroom ideas or things to do at home. Maybe make up two sets of cards.

A DAY WITH DAD OR MOM

Pretend you and your dad or your mom could spend a day all by yourselves. Where would you go? What would you do? What would you talk about? Would you laugh and share some happy memories? Write a story about this special day on a rainbow.

Here is another fun way for children to use their imaginations! They can create pictures with punched out circles from a paper punch.

Have your students punch out lots of circles. They can use one color or several colors. Collect them on a sheet of paper. Then have them glue the circles on a sheet of colored paper. They could create scenes from their favorite stories or fantasize their own scenes.

DREAM BOX

After a class discussion on daydreaming, have each child cover the outside of a box (cube style would be best) with paper or fabric. They could do each side differently if they wanted.

Collect or make items to attach to the box that express their dreams. Use all six sides of the box.

On one side they could write what their dreams are about.

MY PART IN MAKING DREAMS COME TRUE

Have a discussion with your class that dreams really can come true. Have the class help in deciding the method of making them come true.

For example: If one dreams of having wisdom (good grades), then that dream can be fulfilled by studying. Or if one dreams of being popular at school, then that dream can be fulfilled by being kind. Or if one dreams of having friends, then that dream can be fulfilled by being friendly.

FANTASY PUZZLES

Read a story on fantasy to the class. Divide the class into several groups and have each group take a different scene from the story and draw a picture of that scene. Mount on heavy paper.

Cut the pictures into puzzle parts. Keep the pieces in an envelope or box. Have the groups work each other's puzzles. Put the scenes in order after the puzzles are all worked.

UMBRELLA MAZE
Page 11

START

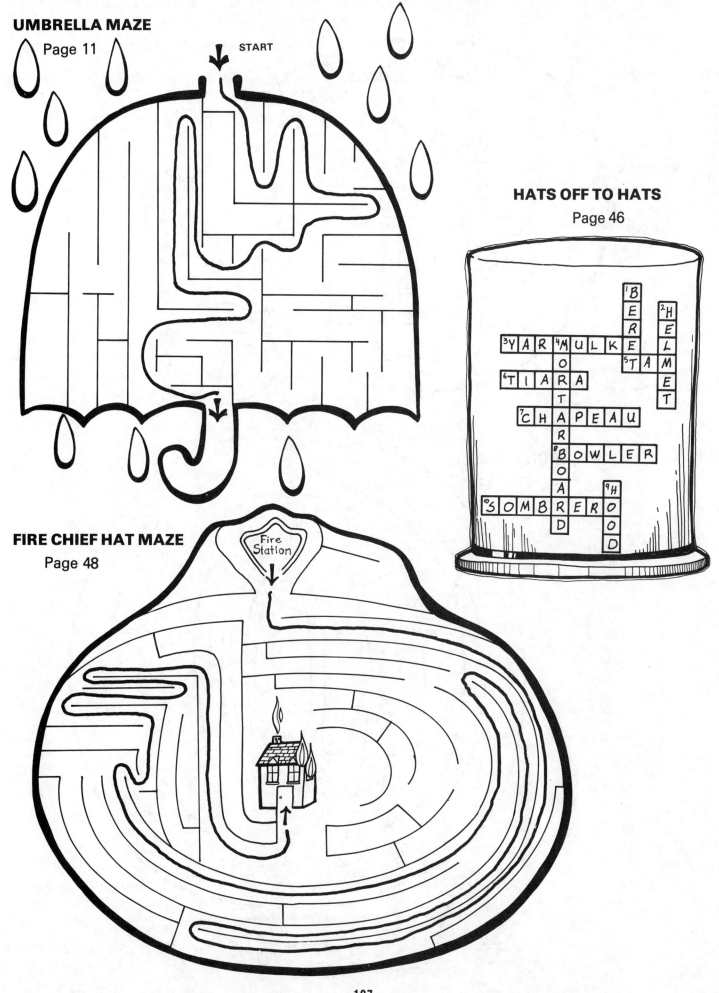

HATS OFF TO HATS
Page 46

₁B E R E ₂H
3Y A R 4M U L K E L
O 5T A M
6T I A R A E
R L
7C H A P E A U M
B E
8B O W L E R T
A
R 9H
10S O M B R E R O O
D O
D

FIRE CHIEF HAT MAZE
Page 48

Fire Station

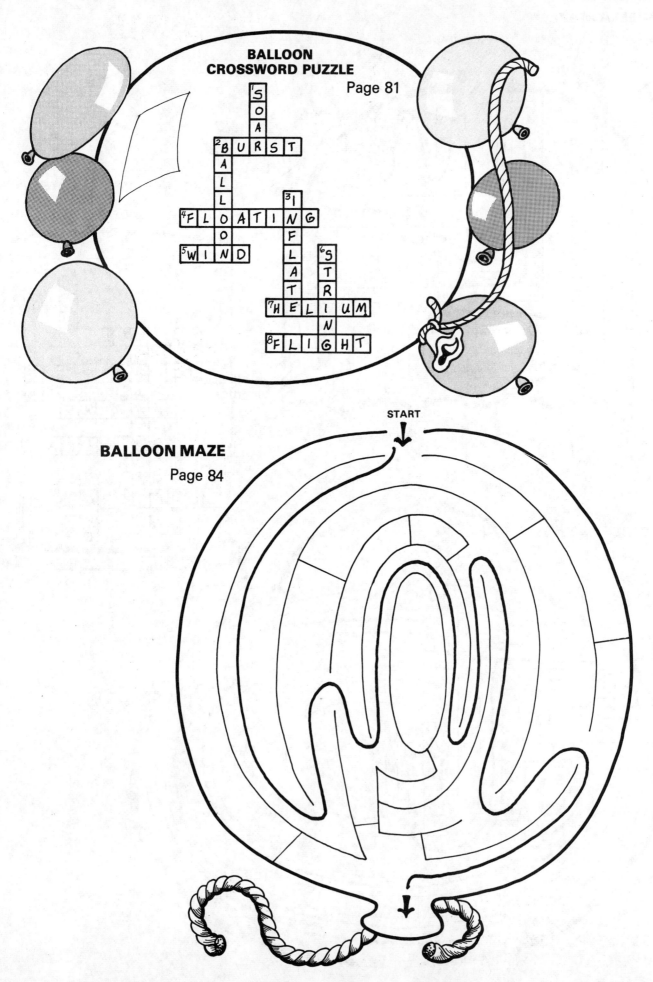

BALLOON
CROSSWORD PUZZLE
Page 81

```
        S
        O
    B U R S T
    A
    L       I
  F L O A T I N G
    O       F
  W I N D   L     S
    O       A     T
            T     R
          H E L I U M
            I     N
          F L I G H T
```

BALLOON MAZE
Page 84

START